06140

JOB SHARING

JOB SHARING
A PRACTICAL GUIDE

Pam Walton

KOGAN
PAGE

Acknowledgements

Thanks to all at New Ways to Work, the job sharers whose experiences are featured and to Kai Dean.

The views expressed are those of the author and not necessarily those of New Ways to Work.

First published in Great Britain in 1990 by Kogan Page Limited, 120 Pentonville Road, London N1 9JN.

British Library Cataloguing in Publication Data

A CIP record for this book is available from the British Library.

ISBN 0-7494-0004-8

Typeset by The Castlefield Press, Wellingborough, Northants.
Printed and bound in Great Britain by
Richard Clay, The Chaucer Press, Bungay

Contents

Chapter 1

Job Sharing: The Background

Work, however defined, plays a central role in our lives and the 1990s could witness significant changes in the way jobs and work are organised. The traditional pattern of nine to five, five days a week, 48 weeks a year and over 48 years does not suit the needs of a large proportion of the working population. Individuals, seeking more balance in their lives, are making demands on employers to change the way that working time is organised. Employers, faced with skills shortages and declining numbers of school leavers, are realising that they will have to make these changes or they may not be able to keep or attract staff.

We describe ourselves in terms of the paid work we do: our status and purpose in life are often closely tied up in our jobs. However, one man, explaining how he felt when he started to job share, says: 'I thought my self-esteem would be undermined, that I'd lose my sense of identity, because I felt my value so much in terms of work. Far from it, I have gained through a much closer relationship with my children.'

Full-time jobs are still seen as the norm, yet only a little more than half (16 million) the workforce of 28 million work full time for an employer. Over five million people work part time, three million are self-employed and two million are registered unemployed. Thus almost half the workforce does not fit this stereotype. A recent report for the Equal Opportunities Commission, 'The under-utilisation of women in the labour market', estimates that six million women of working age – nearly one-third of the age group – are not in paid work.

Work and having a job are not always the same thing. A lot of work is not recognised by pay. Even if you don't have a paid job, work still has a big impact on your life. Women working at home, caring for family members of all ages have not had the status of workers: they are not part of the formal economy and do not earn money for what they do. However, the formal economy relies heavily on their role in domestic, unpaid work. Even if they have full-time, paid jobs outside the home, they still carry out the vast

3

majority of domestic work as well.

A European Commission survey in all member countries in 1985 found that for almost half the workers in Europe, actual working hours and desirable working hours do not coincide. Over one-third (35 per cent) would like to work shorter hours than they do now provided the hourly pay remains the same; 38 per cent considered that no change should be made to the system of working the same number of hours per day, but almost the same number again would prefer to allocate an agreed monthly number of working hours among the individual working days – depending on their own needs and those of their employers. One in six employees would, given the choice, even plump for the still more flexible form of a yearly number of working hours. A new European Commission survey, carried out in 1989 found that 36 per cent of workers would forgo an increase in income in the next pay round in return for shorter average working time.

A survey of almost 26,000 people by the *Guardian* newspaper in October 1988 found that 35 per cent of adults questioned considered flexible working hours likely to be important in their decisions about work in the future – more important than increases in pay, pension schemes and early retirement. This figure included 43 per cent of women and 31 per cent of men.

Combining paid work and family commitments has generally been seen as something of a personal concern rather than of interest to employers or a matter for public policy. The availability of maternity, paternity and parental leave together with childcare provision are vital issues in assisting working parents, as are the availability of reduced and more flexible working hours.

Why are employers considering job sharing and other flexible working arrangements? The last ten years has witnessed a period of rising unemployment and much concern over the decreasing amount of work available for those looking for jobs. During this period there was an upsurge in interest in job sharing within the context of work sharing. The government's Job Splitting Scheme, introduced in 1983, and announced the previous year, was a clear attempt at work sharing.

The situation is changing fast. In July 1988 a National Economic Development Office (NEDO) report predicted that by 1995 the number of 16–19 year olds would drop by almost a quarter. However, the report also found that six out of seven employers were either unaware of these demographic changes or had seriously underestimated them. New research by NEDO published in October 1989, based on a survey of 2,000 firms, finds that employers are over-optimistic about their ability to compete in attracting young people, and too few are trying to adapt their employment practices in order to tap alternative labour forces.

Although the number of young people joining the labour market will fall, at the same time the actual size of the working population will continue to grow. By 1995 there will be one million fewer 19–24 year olds in the labour force, but two million more 25–59 year olds. Employers are being urged to consider recruiting from groups of unemployed job seekers such as women returners, mature workers, people from ethnic minorities and those with disabilities. The study looked at what 35 'innovative' firms were doing in response to this situation and found that the key feature is that these firms have been prepared to challenge long-established personnel practices and entrenched attitudes.

It is being increasingly recognised that within this context, working patterns will need to change. There is nothing God-given about the 35- to 40-hour working week; the tasks of every job do not fit neatly into 40-hour parcels. Flexible working hours, job sharing, career breaks, sabbaticals and term-time working are all being introduced by some employers. In the long term, more radical change in the way jobs are organised should be possible, with the distinction between full and part time removed and the right to pro-rata pay and conditions however many hours you work.

Although it is largely women who are job sharing, men increasingly want to change the balance of their lives, in particular so that they can be more involved in childcare and domestic work. There is a danger in flexibility being available only for women, with the result that men's working lives, hours of work and the domestic division of labour remain unchanged. It is important that schemes introducing more flexible working arrangements are seen as open to all workers. In the long term, this will enable the relationship between paid and domestic work to change for both men and women. In a speech to the Bow Group of Conservative MPs in October 1989, Norman Fowler, Secretary of State for Employment, said that 'Men should play a bigger role at home, to free their wives to go out to work. This means a change of attitude – namely that bringing up children is a shared responsibility. It is not just the responsibility of the woman.' For this to happen, he said that men would have to accept more family responsibilities, while employers would need to be more flexible about working hours, career breaks and job sharing. What is needed, he pointed out, is a change of attitude not just among employers of women, but also employers of men.

This book aims to provide encouragement to both women and men who want to change their working lives. It gives practical information on how to use job sharing as a way of working reduced hours without losing the status and security usually associated with full-time jobs.

Chapter 2

Why Job Share?

What is different about job sharing?

Job sharing is a way of working where two people voluntarily share the responsibilities of one full-time job, dividing the pay, holidays and other benefits between them according to the numbers of hours worked; in other words, each person holds a permanent part-time post. Job sharing is a way of opening up jobs that have previously only been available on a full-time basis to people who want or need to work fewer hours. In theory, all jobs could be considered as available on either a full-time or a job-sharing basis. As one employer put it, 'Never assume that job sharing cannot take place; look at each job and its component parts before making that decision.'

Job sharing is one way of improving the quality and availability of part-time work. One in five workers in the UK now works part time; 90 per cent are women and 85 per cent of these are married women. Overall, 42 per cent of female employees are part-time workers. For many married women, the most convenient and sometimes the only way of combining employment with family responsibilities is to take a part-time job. However, part-time work is generally characterised by low pay, job insecurity, poor promotion prospects and an absence of fringe benefits; it is also concentrated in certain sectors of employment.

Women who take part-time work because of family commitments often take a job which is below their level of skill or qualification; their pay and job status may drop because part-time work is not available in those fields in which they are qualified and/or experienced. A large-scale government survey (*Women and Employment: a lifetime perspective*, HMSO, 1984) found that 45 per cent of women returning part time do so to a job in a lower occupational category than their last job before childbirth.

Although job sharers are fundamentally people working on a part-time basis, job sharing offers a way of increasing access to professional, skilled and rewarding work for those wanting to work part time.

'I didn't particularly want to job share, but to work part-time to pursue other interests. However, this was one of the few 'part-time jobs' in a professional capacity.' (*Job-sharing librarian*)

Two sisters outline how job sharing a clerical post helped them to improve their job prospects.

'When we decided to job share, Angela was an out-of-work housewife and mother, and I was working part time in the village supermarket during school hours; this job was very tiring and paid very low wages. Angela had to give up her job in a supermarket a couple of months earlier because the hours did not fall in school time, and there was no longer anybody to look after her children while she was at work. We noticed from the local council's job advertisements that they operated a job-sharing scheme, so we decided to apply for a full-time job, stating on the application form that we wanted to carry it out on a job-sharing basis. After an interview we were offered the job. The most important thing about job sharing for us is that while I am at work she looks after the children and vice versa, which means that the children are looked after by someone they know and love and we do not have to hand over half our earnings to a child-minder.'

A survey of 175 job sharers carried out by research student, Mary Pritchard, for New Ways to Work in September 1988 found that an overwhelming consensus confirmed the view that job sharing was different from part-time work. Reasons given included: the shared nature of this form of working which meant teamwork, partner support, joint responsibility for decisions, less isolation, etc; job sharing is of higher status than most part-time jobs, opens up more senior jobs and is taken more seriously; better conditions – especially job security and access to training; better career progression; job sharing means more responsibility, greater commitment and is more rewarding and satisfying than part-time work.

It is important to avoid any confusion between the terms 'job sharing' and 'work sharing'. Work sharing is a term used to describe attempts to alleviate the impact of rising unemployment by spreading a reduced volume of work among an existing workforce.

Job sharing was first promoted in the UK by a group of women community workers who formed the Job Share Project in 1977. They were all concerned at the lack of opportunities for well-paid part-time work in the areas they were qualified in. All were parents who wanted to continue in their careers, but on a part-time basis, and they saw the idea of job sharing as one way of doing this. Following articles in the national press featuring examples of job shares at this time, the project (run by one woman from her living room) was inundated with requests for its four-page leaflet.

During the next three years, the project consisted of an informal network of people interested in promoting job sharing; there were regular meetings, but no office or paid workers. In 1980, the Equal Opportunities Commission (EOC) provided funding for the research and publication of two job-sharing guides, one for employees and one for employers. In 1981, the project changed its name to New Ways to Work and established a London office with paid staff. It was funded initially by the Greater London Council and since 1986 by the London Boroughs Grants Unit. It has pioneered the development of job sharing (see p. 139).

Reasons for job sharing

Full-time work does not suit everyone, and job sharing was initially used mainly by women who saw it as opening up the possibility of continuing in reasonably paid work while bringing up children. It is still a means of enabling women and men who want to combine paid work with childcare to do so. Job sharing also provides a positive option for others who do not easily fit into the full-time mould: women or men responsible for caring for elderly or disabled relatives, people with certain disabilities, older workers who want to ease themselves into retirement gradually, people who do not want or need full-time employment for a variety of reasons, such as study or other interests.

Women as job sharers
In the EOC survey of 24 shared jobs (1980), 78 per cent of the sharers were women, and almost three-quarters were under 40 years old. Over a third of sharers looked after children as their main activity during the time they were not working; just over half were involved in community work, study or writing. Mary Pritchard's more recent survey found that 88 per cent were women, and 80 per cent were under 40. The majority of job sharers had dependent children (76 per cent). The reasons most frequently given for wanting to job share were 'better balance between home and work' (71 per cent) and 'responsibility for young children' (67 per cent). More than one reason was given in the majority of cases. Other reasons included

self-employment (8 per cent), studying (7 per cent), health problems (3 per cent), responsibility for elderly dependants (3 per cent), and preparation for retirement (1 per cent).

The majority of women returning to employment after a break for childbearing do so part time, but the convenience of working part time is often bought at a cost: that of returning to lower pay and status. A survey carried out in 1982 by Leicester City Council of female employees who had left their employment for maternity reasons found that out of 40 women, 33 would be looking to return to work on a part-time basis. The council responded to this by drawing up a job-share scheme.

Increasingly, women who take maternity leave but do not want to return on a full-time basis are successfully negotiating return on a job-share basis. There is no statutory entitlement to flexibility or reduction in working hours to accommodate family responsibilities; but in a number of cases, the refusal by an employer to allow a woman to alter or reduce her hours of working has been held by tribunals to constitute indirect discrimination in certain circumstances (see Chapter 9). Only women, however, can currently gain access to job sharing in this way. One early tribunal ruling (Holmes *v* Home Office) decided that the Home Office unlawfully discriminated against a women civil servant on the grounds of her sex, by refusing to allow her to work part-time after the birth of her child. This decision encouraged growing numbers of employers, particularly in the public sector, to allow women to return part time after maternity leave.

One woman who did return full time after maternity leave eventually found that job sharing was the answer to her stressful situation. Sheila McPhee returned to work as a senior manager for British Telecom.

> 'It's a very demanding job and I felt I was not performing as well as I did before. In the end I worked full time for nine months, and over that period I felt more and more stressed and less and less able to cope with the double life. I was rapidly coming to the conclusion that the only option was to resign and to perhaps have a few years away from work altogether.'

Sheila and a colleague who was about to have a baby negotiated a job share and now, while their mothers share a job, the children share a nursery place at City Child Nursery.

Another pair who negotiated to share a deputy community librarian post after maternity leave found that they were conveniently expecting babies 10 days apart.

Two women explain more fully why they decided to job share:

'I have a little girl of nearly 18 months and although I feel the need to work, I want to be with her as much as possible while she needs me. I currently enjoy working 17½ hours only per week. Also it means I can get out and about and have more time for personal interests, too. It's ideal. If I'm honest, I never was very keen on the idea of working five days a week. I'd much rather have half the money and more time to live my own life after work – yet at the same time I do very much enjoy my 2½ working days – often finding that I'm thinking about different ideas/projects to do with work when I'm at home. I can't stress too much just how ideal a situation a job share is for me. (*Administration and Information Officer in a local authority*)

'The thing about doing job share rather than working part time – I mean, there are lots of part-time jobs in teaching – is that the job was a promotion for me, and gave me a higher salary, so it's an improvement while remaining part time. My husband and I have both job shared, when the children were young.' (*Teacher in a North London infants school*)

An increasing option for men

More men are now considering job sharing as a way in which they can play a more active role in taking responsibility for their children. As one male job sharer commented, 'I've gained a fantastic amount by not being a working father, always out of the house.' Some married couples have turned to job sharing as a way of sharing parenting and enabling both to have jobs outside the home. New Ways to Work have gathered information from 21 couples who use job sharing in this way. The potential of job sharing to help couples who want to combine careers and child raising is illustrated by a couple who share a job as sub-editor on a national newspaper.

'The idea of job sharing occurred to us soon after we got together, well before our daughter came along. We thought it would suit us, because we wanted to have children and we wanted to look after them between us.'

Linda Gregory and John Randall shared a job as Principal Social Worker for Sheffield City Council; they also shared the care of their two children aged three and six:

'We both felt that we didn't see much point in having the children if we were going to get other people to care for them quite a lot, particularly when they were small. It's our personal view – we felt that we wanted to take a lot of care of them, and it seemed ideal. It has been a very good solution for us, because it's allowed us both to do that. I think people thought it was a bit strange for a man – it was like John giving up any ambition. But now they see that John has obviously enjoyed being at home with the kids and having time with them, and that the children have a very good relationship with him. However, it's interesting that some men who say they have a commitment to childcare say, under pressure, that they themselves wouldn't want to do what we do.

'I think the children benefit from the fact that the times that I am at home I'm positively wanting to be at home, and to be with them, and the same goes for John. They've the two of us – we're very different, we do different things with the children – so they have different experiences, different relationships, and I think it's been good for them and for us. Both children will ask "Who's looking after us today?" Usually as long as they know, they're fine – but they like to know.

'I'm not sure how long we'll go on job sharing. One thing is the money. Although we do slightly better as job sharers because of the tax allowance, as the children get bigger and the demands on money get larger, I don't know then whether we'd want one of us to go full time. I'm not sure. Now that Laura's old enough to start playgroup, I'm thinking of doing some research. We've been very satisfied with the arrangement, although I appreciate it's not the solution for everyone.'

To many of these couples, the principal motivation for job sharing is the importance they attach to playing an equal role in bringing up their children. One commented:

'I've seen relationships in which couples have been working for years and they've been more or less equal, but as soon as they've had children the woman has remained at home and has geared the rest of her life to her husband's career.'

Another added that:

'We feel job sharing is not only a contribution to a balanced way of life, but also a significant way of producing some day-to-day equality between male and female roles.'

Single parents

Single parents may benefit too, as long as the full-time wage is high enough. One single parent found that although it was difficult to manage on the income from her job share, she felt it would be detrimental to her daughter if she worked full time. A single parent who shared a job as a nurse in the Greater London Council's medical centre commented:

> 'Sharing has meant I have been able to come back to work much earlier than I expected. My children are 1½ and 3½ and I think we will all benefit. They will have someone else in their lives and it will be good for me to get away. As a single parent I won't earn more than I can get on Social Security but working is necessary for me. I don't think it is right to be closeted at home 24 hours a day. Job sharing gives me time for myself and my home as well as stimulation and it will make it much easier to return to full-time work later.'

Women returners

For many women who have already left paid jobs for childcare and other domestic reasons, job sharing can ease the transition back into the job market after years at home. One job sharer previously worked at a senior level in housing, but then spent seven years looking after children full time. She wrote to ten housing associations about the possibility of a job share but was eventually successful in obtaining a shared post with a local authority. She is very pleased with this and doesn't mind the fact that it is at a lower level than previously, as she feels that having been out of touch for seven years, she needs to build up her confidence and knowledge again.

Carers

Job sharing can also enable people with caring responsibilities for elderly or disabled relatives to continue in paid employment. A recent government report (Green, Hazel, 'Informal Carers', HMSO, 1988) estimated that there are six million informal carers in Great Britain. An increase of nearly 90 per cent in the number of people aged over 85 between 1986 and 1996 is also predicted. Thus many more employees will have caring responsibilities for the elderly.

Successive governments have been turning towards the notion of 'care in the community'. The Griffiths report 'Community Care: Agenda for Action' 1988 makes it clear that families will continue to be the main providers of care, and the Equal Opportunities Commission in responding to this report suggests that 'employers develop policies which allow these employees with caring responsibilities to combine their work and caring responsibilities'.

People with disabilities

Job sharing can also be a creative and positive way for people with disabilities to work to their full potential. Not all want to be typists, telephonists or gardeners – traditional jobs for those with disabilities. In June 1984, Leeds City Council considered a report on job sharing which suggested that full-time work could sometimes be too strenuous for people with disabilities and recommended job sharing as an important equal opportunities measure.

A woman sharing the post of Head of the Disability Unit for Hackney Council confirms this.

'Both myself and my job sharer have disabilities and wanted to work less than a 35-hour week because of physical limits on energy due to disability.'

Another job sharer has multiple sclerosis and would get too tired to do a full-time job.

Time for other interests

Job sharing may also be appropriate for people who have other interests to pursue and who want to lead a more varied and balanced life; for one job sharer it was 'a conscious decision to opt for a lower material standard of living: time is more valuable than money. Job sharing is one of the few ways of making more time to develop other talents, yet maintain and even enhance the interest and satisfaction of one's present job.' To some, job sharing can provide the opportunity to study, like the person on a part-time librarianship course who shares a job in a library, or to carry out research. Angela Heslop, who job shares a ward sister's post at Charing Cross Hospital, carries out research at the hospital during the other half of the week.

Twin brothers shared a job as picture-framer at a gallery in Norfolk on an alternate week basis, and in their 'week off' worked on their own paintings. Bob Payne, who shares a Principal Social Worker post in Sheffield, also runs a 31-acre farm.

'One day I'm making silage and worrying about whether the tractor is going to break down and the next I'm trying to decide if a child in care should be returned to its parents.'

His job sharer, Margaret Wood, wanted more time to pursue further education. Lorraine Baker shared a clerical job with GEC Tele-communications in 1984 to enable her to pursue her athletics career.

Part Time Careers Ltd, an agency which provides permanent part-time work for experienced office workers, say they receive a lot of interest from creative or artistic people; these have included a trumpet player, a novelty cake-maker, a dressage enthusiast and an opera singer. In February 1988, Valerie Masterson and Anne Mackay shared the demanding lead role in an operetta at Sadlers Wells on alternate nights.

New Ways to Work received a request for help from a man who was a computer analyst/programmer as well as a vicar choral in the choir at the local cathedral. He explains:

> 'Doing both jobs is very tiring, and does not leave much time for riding my horse (which is the most important thing in my life). For this reason I would very much like to share a job with another person.'

A journalist who shares his job as sub-editor on a national newspaper and devotes the rest of his time to family life and landscape photography comments:

> 'Life wouldn't be worth living if I couldn't take my photographs, and I'm finding increasingly that it would be impossible if I had to in any way return to a full-time journalistic career.'

His job sharer spends the rest of his time pursuing an acting career and says:

> 'Job sharing is extremely important to me because it enables me to pursue two different careers at the same time, which wouldn't be possible otherwise.'

Don MacDonald shared a job as training manager at the Stock Exchange while also working part of the week as a lecturer in management, a job which he had done full time for eight years. He comments:

> 'I felt this was an opportunity to get back into a management job and practise it rather than just talk about it.'

For jobs with high stress levels, job sharing can help to reduce 'burn-out'. One woman, after ten years as a senior manager in the health service, had begun to tire of working nights and weekends, clocking up 80 hours a week; her personal life was being destroyed by the long hours. She now shares the job of Unit General Manager for Camberwell Health Authority's mental and community health services, and both she and her partner say they now feel fresher at work and that normality has been restored to their personal lives.

In the USA, the use of job sharing as a way of easing people into retirement is more widespread than in the UK, and a number of companies offer workers this option. When British Telecom announced their job-share scheme in early 1989 in an effort to retain women workers, the union official in charge of the negotiations said that some sections of the union's main engineering group had shown increasing interest in the agreement as a way of providing a flexible route into retirement. Hackney Council, at the suggestion of the craft unions, have changed their pension arrangements and linked their job-share scheme with early retirement (see Chapter 10).

Chapter 3

What Jobs Are Shared?

Only ten years ago it was hard to find many examples of shared jobs. The Equal Opportunities Commission survey of 1980 found only 28 pairs of job sharers to whom they could send a questionnaire; 24 replied. The range of jobs included: library work; lecturing; administration; medicine; research; planning; housing; community/advice/social work; TV production work. Pritchard found that 21 per cent of jobs fell into the managerial/high level administrative category, followed by education (14 per cent), community work (13 per cent), social work and probation (11 per cent) and librarianship (10 per cent).

The list of jobs shared is now fairly extensive. This chapter illustrates the range and gives more detailed information on some types of employment where job sharing is widespread. New Ways to Work can provide more detailed information.

Teaching

Both the number of teaching job shares and education authorities with job share policies is increasing steadily. Preliminary results of a survey carried out by June Smedley at Loughborough University in 1988–89 show that 15 of the 100 authorities responding to the survey had formal job share schemes, six expect to start them during the current academic year, and another 22 were considering the idea. A further 28 had informal arrangements. Five schemes were studied in greater depth and 170 head teachers with experience of job sharing were asked for their views. Just over half of the 58 per cent in favour were 'very positive', 24 per cent were neutral and 19 per cent were negative. Although the majority of sharers were on the main professional grade, some were in promoted posts including several shared head of department posts and two shared deputy head posts.

During the 1960s, schools experienced acute teacher shortages and became heavily dependent on part-time staff; some teachers were in practice, if not in name, actually sharing classes. However, by the end of the 1970s part-time teaching opportunities had been greatly reduced and were on the whole restricted to the lowest scale (scale one).

In January 1982 Sheffield Education Authority, concerned with the growing number of unemployed teachers, invited them and other education staff to apply for job-sharing posts; 40 teachers responded. The most contentious issue in the early days was whether job-sharing teachers could hold posts above the lowest level. In July 1982, a one-day conference for teachers wanting to job share was held in London and this was followed by the setting up of a London Teachers' job-sharing group. This group was very active in pushing the Inner London Education Authority (ILEA) into accepting job sharing. Joan Nicholson and Mike Trier became the first job sharers for a pilot year in 1982. Following a further successful pilot scheme involving 70 posts, from September 1986 ILEA implemented a full job-share scheme for teachers, with all full-time, permanent posts open to job sharing, except for head and deputy head.

It is now possible to hold a responsible, high-level job in teaching on a job-share basis. Jane Leggatt and Andrew Bethell job share as Head of Sixth Form at Stoke Newington Sixth Form Centre (such posts are no longer excluded from the job-share scheme) and for the last four years Richard Patterson and Terry Little have shared the job of Head of Information Technology at a comprehensive school in Birkenhead.

Maureen Coles and Sue Hadfield share a job at a secondary school in East Sussex. Maureen says:

> 'I like the regular work. With part-time teaching, you don't know if you will have a job the next year. You also feel part of the school, and the school sees you differently. You can feel very lonely and isolated as a teacher, but we have someone we can discuss things with.'

They put the idea to the head when one was working on a temporary full-time contract and the other was coming in for odd days to cover for staff sickness. One unexpected difficulty, as Sue explains, was:

> 'I was very surprised at just how possessive I felt about the kids I teach. I'm very proud of them, but I've always tended to think of them as mine. I'm still proud of them, but they're not my kids any more – they're ours.'

Some of the teaching job sharers are men, with a few 'couples'. One male sharer commented that 'the governors were "prepared" to let me job share, but didn't think it to be very manly'. Another said:

> 'It's harder for men to job share, there are all sorts of hidden pressures. There's a feeling that if a man doesn't have a full-time job there's something not quite right, whereas it's becoming accepted practice for a woman.'

Although it has become easier to obtain a shared teaching job in parts of the country, it can be difficult to convince some heads that more senior jobs can be shared. The fact that some local education authorities are agreeing more formal job share policies helps this situation. However, there are fears that the local management of schools may set the clock back. Kate Myers, writing in *'Education'* in June 1989, raised concerns about the fact that governors of schools will be responsible for recruiting teachers, but the LEA will remain the employer and as such answerable at industrial tribunals. Governors will want 'the best' and most cost-effective option for their pupils. They may decide that career breaks and job share schemes are just not feasible for units of their size.

Lecturing

Lecturer jobs in universities, polytechnics, further and higher education colleges have been shared; these include an English lecturer at Manchester Polytechnic; lecturer in architecture at Sheffield University; lecturer in social sciences in higher education; Head of Art at an art college.

Sarah and James Coakley started sharing their job as Religious Studies Lecturer at Lancaster University in 1977. Because they have different specialisms they teach different courses. They did have problems, with each of their workloads ending up as more than half of a full-time job. They explain:

> 'With lecturing, it's very difficult to assess how hard people are working; it was revealed that in some years we had been doing twice as much as we should.'

Library work

Part-time work has long been available within libraries, but only at low levels and with no prospects for promotion. One woman who shares a job as a school librarian explains:

'If we were to work part time, it would be as library assistants and all we'd be doing is shelving and issuing books. This way we've got the professional duties and responsibilities as well.'

There are now many examples of shared librarian posts. These include: subject librarian in a polytechnic; information scientist for a private company; health authority librarian; children's librarian; many librarians in public libraries, at all levels, including branch librarian. The House of Commons first employed job sharers in the post of Senior Library Clerk in 1972 and this was so successful that the arrangements were expanded, so that by 1987 there were 12 shared jobs at senior and junior levels.

Shirley Tunley and Claire Bayliss have shared a job as librarian at the Welsh Agricultural College in Aberystwyth since 1983. Getting this job share agreed was not easy: it took Shirley, who originally held the job full time, years to obtain agreement. The other half was then advertised in the local press and Jobcentre, and as a result there were 40 applications (Aberystwyth only has a population of 12,000). Shirley and Claire work half the week each, with an overlap time on Wednesday to meet and talk. Although they share a lot of their work they also have their own special fields. They see as a bonus the fact that they can both go to a meeting on the same day. Another bonus, particularly when working with the public and doing long hours, is that you don't lose your edge or enthusiasm and you have time to keep up with the latest trends.

Maureen Pascoe and Barbara Sorby have been job sharing since 1982, originally as Senior Library Assistant. In 1984 they jointly obtained promotion to Central Children's Librarian.

'As well as supervising the service, dealing with stock selection and all the admin, there's a lot of work to be done in the community – like running a parent's information centre, organising book launches for local authors, workshops and sessions with children's artists.'

Because the work is so varied and requires a constant input of ideas, two different brains are a positive advantage. They can bounce ideas off each other and take a much broader approach. The lack of a rigid routine and constant evening work mean that Barbara and Maureen work a totally flexible system of hours, which could cause problems if they didn't work so well together. The service needs 37 hours a week and between them they make sure it gets it. They are meticulous about their professionalism: they split the week into two and a half days each if there are no special events, but their timetable is prepared and circulated to other departments a week, often a month, in advance.

Perhaps the greatest bonus of the arrangement has been the mutual support that has developed. Over the years they have become good friends, outside as well as inside work. For their present job, they both wrote individual letters of application. Putting them together, they found they were complementary: one had written about the methods they would use to share, while the other had covered the philosophy of sharing and how it works. Barbara says:

> 'When we have had problems in the past the fact that there's always someone to discuss the problem with has kept me going.'

As part of their studies for a degree in librarianship they undertook a joint project on job sharing. This was published in 1982 as 'Job sharing: the great divide' by Leeds Polytechnic.

The fact that job sharers can improve evening and Saturday coverage in libraries can be an advantage. However, as a children's librarian in Wandsworth points out:

> 'While our job-sharing timetable provides the branch with better coverage of the children's library (all five evenings, at least three out of four Saturdays, and at least part of any week of annual leave), it does mean extremely complicated time-tabling chores for the librarian.'

Although there are a number of shared branch librarian posts, Marilyn Clymo, who wanted to share her job in Wandsworth, was unable to do so. While agreeing to job sharing up to deputy level, the libraries' management would not allow Marilyn's branch librarian post to be shared. She took her case to an industrial tribunal under the Sex Discrimination Act, and unfortunately lost. She left her job, and her husband, who she had originally wanted to share with, was appointed to her post (see Chapter 9).

For anyone wanting to job share in library work, there are many positive examples to point to and the Library Association has produced a pamphlet on job sharing for members.

Planning

Part-time work in planning has been hard to find. In a short article in *'Planning'* newspaper in 1979, only one example of a job share was found, in Westminster City Council. More recently there has been a growth in the number of shared planning posts. Job sharers have been employed by Staffordshire County, Bolton, Rochdale, St Albans, Leicester, Central Regional Council and a number of the London boroughs, the Town and Country Planning Association and at Planning Aid for Londoners. Jobs are shared at all levels including a number at principal officer level in local authorities. However there are still cases of planners being unsuccessful in convincing managers that jobs at higher levels can be shared. The Royal Town Planning Institute operates a job share register and has produced an information and contact sheet for members on job sharing.

Frances Wheat and Maggie Jones shared the post of Principal Planning Officer grade PO2 at Westminster City Council for two years. Frances had previously worked for the council full time for seven years. After taking maternity leave she was successful in negotiating to job share; the half post was advertised and there were nine applicants. Frances was not on the selection panel but she met all the interviewees and the panel asked her for her opinion. When asked to provide the panel with guidelines, she stressed that they were interviewing for one united job-share post, not two separate part-time jobs. Maggie Jones was appointed and for almost three years Maggie and Frances worked from the same desk and shared the same diary. Frances explains:

> 'We took the "lead" on different projects and kept up to date with each other's work, so that we could always cover for one another. We worked alternate days so that there was never more than one day before the "lead" on a particular project was in again. In addition, we kept a "day book" system of informing each other of any interesting discussions, telephone calls etc. It worked extremely smoothly, to the extent that people forgot which one of us they had spoken to or we alternately redrafted committee reports where necessary.'

Prompted by reorganisation at Westminster and a need for new challenges, Frances and Maggie decided to move on together. Over a period of a few months they applied for three posts, attended three interviews and obtained one job offer. Since September 1987, they have worked as Principal Planning Officer (PO4) for the London

Borough of Hillingdon, as part of a team of professional experts working on action-orientated project work within the Implementation Section. They are given a high degree of responsibility and initiative, organise their work on a project basis and are prepared to cover for each other. Their management function includes supervision of one other principal officer and ad hoc management in relation to specific projects.

Their partnership is clearly a success. Maggie explains:

'You need motivation and commitment to make it work, together with loyalty to the partnership; this, in our case, involves a similar approach to work and compatible personalities. I'm not saying that only one partnership will work for one person, but that the right ingredients have to be there, as in any team.'

Between them, Frances and Maggie have 34 years' experience as qualified town planners. In December 1989 they were again promoted together.

Landscape architecture

Susan and Kate shared a job as a landscape architect for Greater Manchester Council. They each had different projects to work on, and space was made for them both to have their own special equipment, drawing boards etc. They were together in the office one morning a week. Other posts have been shared in Newcastle upon Tyne and Bury Councils.

Personnel and training

Only two or three years ago it was very rare to see job share personnel posts advertised, but it is now becoming more commonplace. An early example of a job share was that of Senior Training Officer at the Stock Exchange, which was first shared in 1981. Jean Lammiman and Don MacDonald shared this job for a number of years and together received promotion to Training Manager. They found that in a creative job such as theirs, the opportunity to bounce ideas off each other was a major benefit. They also found it useful on occasions to be able to run courses together. Two distinct sets of skills and experience were made available to the Stock Exchange, which added significantly to the range of activities they could cover.

Another training post shared is that of Senior Training Officer for the Federation of Jewish Family Services.

Carolyn Altounyan and Angela Probart job share as Assistant Personnel Officer for Sheffield City Council. They had previously worked full time together in the same section, and went on maternity leave at similar times. Other posts shared include Lay Training Officer for the Diocese of Southwark, equal opportunities adviser, Calderdale Borough, and a personnel officer for a health authority. Westminster City Council have two job-sharing personnel officers responsible for the job share scheme. The retail division of Boots employs personnel officers sharing a job in Swansea.

Social work

Many social worker posts are shared at various levels. One level three social worker describes how the job was shared:

> 'We had separate caseloads, and we agreed that we would cover for the other person in their half of the week, but we rarely got called out. You told people when you would be in the office and they usually accepted that. Occasionally, people wanted to test out how you would respond if they had a problem, or if there was a genuine emergency that they needed help with, or you had to investigate something. It worked well – no problems at all; clients seemed quite happy with it. They had you all the time, but they knew that if there was a problem, there was someone else available to cover who had a little bit of knowledge – not usually very much, but a bit. The reactions from colleagues were very positive and supportive. We're quite different as people and as workers; they seemed to feel they could relate to both of us, and nobody seemed to have any problems with that. We also supervised students. One of us would take responsibility for writing their reports and doing their supervision on a weekly level, and the other would help them on a day-to-day basis, settle them in etc.'

A husband-and-wife pair, Owen and Susie Gill, who shared a job with Avon Social Services in the late seventies, describe the particular advantages of sharing rather than working part time. They shared an intake social worker post in a busy central Bristol office.

'The question we are most often asked is whether we share the same clients – in other words, whether we carry simply one caseload. The answer is that we each have our individual clients as any part-timer would, but we also keep a "watching brief" on the cases of the other, on the days he/she is not working. It occasionally happens that we get involved with our partner's cases, if work flows into the following day. For instance, if one of us admits an elderly person to a residential place, the chances are that the other will have some involvement the following day, completing the work. The arrangement of the "watching brief" on the other's cases also has the effect of countering the criticism of part-timers – often overstated – that they are not available when there is a crisis on one of their cases. In other words, if for instance children on one of our caseloads have to come into care as an emergency on one of their non-working days, the other would automatically consider it as his/her responsibility to be involved.'

When New Ways to Work carried out its survey of local authorities in 1987, it found that Sheffield Family and Community Services Department had 51 posts shared within the department; thorough counselling was given to those considering job sharing, and the scheme was well known throughout the department. Nottinghamshire County Council also had a well-developed scheme in its Social Services Department, with 34 shared posts. The personnel officer responsible for job sharing within the department had taken positive measures to inform managers about the initiative. He commented:

'One considerable asset seems to be that provided staff are amenable, job sharers can work on the same day, thus doubling up staff numbers for special events, for example group outings, special projects etc.'

Community work

A wide range of community work jobs have been shared. A group of women community workers first started the Job Share Project (now New Ways to Work) in 1977 to promote the idea of job sharing. Community work jobs are shared in many local authorities around the country. There is also a wide variety of jobs shared in voluntary organisations; these have included resource worker at a community resource centre in Milton Keynes, organiser for Riversdale

Community Centre in Norfolk, neighbourhood worker with the elderly for a residents' association in Birmingham, co-operative development worker for Southwark Co-operative Development Agency, fieldworker for the National Cyrenians, development officer for Leominster District Community Association, fieldworker for International Voluntary Service and co-ordinator for a Crossroads Care Attendant Scheme.

Probation officers

Penny Neale and Sarah Kershaw started sharing their probation officer post with the Inner London Probation Service in 1981 and were closely monitored as part of a two-year experiment. Now many probation officers in the Inner London Probation Services share jobs; the Greater Manchester Probation Service also has about a dozen shared posts and there are other examples around the country. Anne Burrell and Kate Quaid share in Warwickshire: they specialise in preparing reports for courts and in initial short-term assessments, but they each have their own cases to supervise too.

Housing

Both local authority housing departments and housing associations now employ job sharers in a variety of jobs. The following job-share vacancies have recently appeared in the press:

Finance Worker for Leeds Housing Concern
Supported Housing Manager for Circle 33 Housing Trust
Housing Officer for Notting Hill Housing Trust
Senior Housing Officer – Lettings, for the Metropolitan Housing Trust

Job sharers are also employed by North Sheffield Housing Association and Hyde Housing Association in London. The job of hostel supervisor for St Mungo's Housing Association was shared for two years and that of deputy director at the Co-ordinated Accommodation Scheme has been shared since 1985.

Local authority vacancies include Assistant District Housing Manager and Principal Rehousing Officer for the London Borough of Greenwich. Job sharers have also worked for the Housing Corporation, Liverpool City Council and Leicester City Council. The post of Assistant Chief Housing Officer for Colchester Borough

Council has been shared since March 1988 (see Chapter 3).

The London Branch of the Institute of Housing sent a 'Job sharing and return to work' survey to 84 boroughs and housing associations in London in 1988. The survey found that 13 out of the 41 respondents employed job sharers and a further 10 were developing a job-sharing policy. HERA (Housing Employment Register and Advice) has run seminars for job sharers and managers.

Careers work

In January 1986, two careers officers from Strathclyde Regional Council won the right to share their job at an industrial tribunal (see Chapter 9). Their immediate boss, a supporting witness for them at the tribunal, held the opinion that the basic careers officer's job lends itself particularly well to job sharing.

Jobs shared include careers adviser (higher education) at Kingston-upon-Thames Polytechnic, and careers officer for the London Borough of Richmond upon Thames.

Journalism

Sub-editors, feature writers and reporters are all sharing jobs. The *Financial Times* has job sharers in three sub-editor posts. Jeremy Clyne and Ian Chapman share one of these posts, while another is shared by a husband and wife – Liz Houghton and Alex Skorecki. The job of sub-editor is particularly suited to sharing, as it consists of four nine-hour shifts a week, and all work must be completed by the end of the shift.

Jennifer Cunningham and Anne Johnston share a job as feature writer for the *Glasgow Herald*. They had previously worked full time for the paper and conveniently became pregnant a month apart.

Health workers

The National Health Service is the biggest employer of women in the whole of Europe. Managers of job sharers in the NHS who were contacted by a steering group on equal opportunities for women in the Health Service reported being 'staggered' by the quality of applicants for job-sharing vacancies. They also reported that, although the training may cost more, an in-post sharer can train any 'new half', offsetting some of the training costs; any extra costs incurred by overlap time are more than compensated for by the additional vigour, input, etc of two brains working on the job. The steering group, which was set up by the health minister in 1986, published a resource pack with a section on job sharing, in which they conclude that 'No equal opportunities programme can be complete without the option of job sharing being made available.'

Other shared jobs within the NHS include: radiographers, occupational therapists, hospital pharmacists, medical social worker, laboratory technician. The highest level post is that of Unit General Manager in Camberwell Health Authority (see page 34).

Nursing

In 1986, Angela Heslop and Heidi Lempp became the first two job-sharing ward sisters at Charing Cross Hospital in London, working on a busy medical ward which specialises in respiratory disorders. Between them they had 32 years of experience of nursing and both had previously worked as full-time sisters on the ward. The job share took them eight months of planning and negotiation.

They shared a 37½ hour week, each working 18¾ hours. They found the best way to provide continuity was to work Wednesday to Wednesday, with an overlap period – often half a shift on a Wednesday when they met to discuss matters related to the ward, review policies and plans and make decisions. They also kept a diary and used the telephone to keep in contact with each other. The two sisters shared responsibility for the management of the ward, but remained individually responsible for their actions while on duty. An independent evaluation of their job share was commissioned by their health district, the Riverside Health Authority, and this was published as 'Job sharing a ward sister's post' in 1987. The report states:

> 'On the whole the shared responsibility did not seem to cause problems, but potentially the sharing of responsibility is difficult to achieve effectively. In this case, the ability of the two sisters to agree on their main objectives; to share the power and authority vested in the role; to accept compromise on occasions and to trust each other's judgement were key factors.'

After 18 months Heidi left and was replaced by Sheila Sparrow.

There are now a number of shared sisters' posts; these are stoma care sister at Dudley Road Hospital in Birmingham; Ward Sister, neurosurgery/neuromedical, Southampton General Hospital; a night sister at Bethlem Royal Hospital in Kent; a midwifery sister and seven other midwifery posts at Queen Elizabeth II Hospital in

Welwyn Garden City; a night sister's post at Leicester Royal Infirmary.

Other posts shared include community midwives in East Hertfordshire, a district nursing sister in Leicestershire and a nurse–teacher post in Bromsgrove and Redditch.

Both the Royal College of Nursing and the Royal College of Midwives are keen to promote job sharing.

Health visitors

Maggie Hammarton and Mary Jeffries share a health visitor's job in Essex. They have shared out the hours into one-third/two-thirds; one works three days and one evening and the other one and a half days. They sit down once a month to plan their rota of hours. They say having similar approaches to the work helps: 'If we are dealing with the other's patient we know the sort of advice the other one would give.' They make sure the patients know what's happening and Maggie says none of Mary's families has objected to seeing her instead. They share a desk, but each has a chair.

Acute shortages of health visitors, particularly in rural areas, have encouraged managers to be more open to the idea. Five pairs of sharers are employed by East Suffolk Health Authority and there are a number of other examples, including a pair who have successfully shared in Grantham, Lincolnshire for the last four years.

They don't operate with separate caseloads, but share their clients, finding that neither the clients nor GPs are confused.

General practice

Full-time general medical practice often involves a minimum of 60 hours a week and up to 90 hours. It is estimated that there are between 25 and 30 job-sharing arrangements within general practice.

Dr Gene Felder is a GP who has been job sharing for nearly three years, since the birth of his first child. He shares with Dr Tricia Jenkinson, who is his second job-share partner, at a health centre in Hackney. He explains:

'I work about 23 hours on Tuesday, Thursday and Friday, and my partner on Tuesday, Wednesday and Friday. In addition,

I am on call one night in six and one weekend in six. We share these duties with the other doctors at the health centre. This averages out at about 40 hours a week. The health centre does not keep separate lists for each doctor, but refers patients to the doctor most appropriate for their particular complaint. There's always some problem of continuity of care in a practice, no matter how many hours the doctors work; nobody can be available all the hours of every day.'

Hospital medicine

The Lothian Health Board pioneered the introduction of job sharing for senior registrar and consultant posts; there are currently two shared consultant's posts. Other jobs shared include a senior clinical psychologist at University College Hospital and a child medicine lecturer at Guy's Hospital.

Kate Whitfield and Emma Rowley shared an obstetric house officer job at the Royal Free Hospital for a year. Emma found that obstetrics lends itself well to sharing:

'Things happen so quickly, and at night the hand over is already built into the system.'

They also thought that their patients got better care, as hand-over time acted as a time to think about patient management and as an incentive to get things sorted out. The sharers also think they learnt a lot. Emma says, 'I picked up quite a bit from what she'd written in the notes. Another brain, a different background.'

The British Medical Association runs a job-share register for doctors which attempts to put people who want to share in touch with each other. The form collects details of the speciality, grade and geographical location of prospective sharers. At present there are 98 doctors on the register: 62 seeking hospital appointments, 25 seeking partnerships in general practice and 11 seeking general practice trainee appointments. The Women in Medicine group has produced a short guide on how to achieve a shared GP post, 'Job sharing in General Practice'. It describes how two job-sharing doctors can fit into a practice, what allowances are available, the implications for the practice and the doctors, and the potential problems.

Other examples

There is a range of shared office jobs including posts for clerks, typists, secretaries, administrators and receptionists. Other examples include environmental health officer, home help organiser, nursery nurse, caretaker, gardener, traffic engineer and accountant. The job of Museums Education Officer in Cheltenham was first shared in 1981. The post-holder returned to job share after maternity leave and the other half was advertised. It was still shared seven years later, although partners had changed. As one of the partners explains:

'The benefits of two people being in two places at once were great, catering for two schools at the same time. Working together planning sessions and exhibitions is a great bonus, an exchange of ideas bringing out more thoughts and possibilities.'

How can senior and managerial level jobs be shared?

The job sharers in the Industrial Society study, *Does Job Sharing Work?*, supervised up to seven employees. On the whole, the researchers did not detect major problems in job sharers performing this role, though inevitably having two, often distinct, personalities presented some difficulties. The job sharers themselves were well aware that they needed to co-ordinate this aspect of their work and present a united front.

The research suggested that planning and balancing the workload on subordinates is important. All the employees they contacted saw it as a benefit to have job sharers as appraisal/reporting officers. They felt that job sharers counteracted any bias or prejudice which could arise from having one person evaluating work performance. Some felt they got on with one sharer more than the other, and thought this provided greater security for their own career development. Overall the supervisory role did not emerge as a difficult area, especially in work units which were flexible or team based.

The issues of concern in the sharing of senior and managerial level jobs include problems of management continuity and consistency of approach: that junior staff will have difficulties with two bosses and that junior staff will play one off against the other. These are all real fears and it is essential that job sharing managers work out a strategy for them. There will be a need for clear lines of communication and a regular overlap time. However, none of these difficulties is impossible to overcome, as has been demonstrated by the increasing numbers of jobs shared at these levels.

Only three years ago it was hard to find examples of jobs being shared at senior levels; the most senior jobs were a hospital consultant and the training manager at the Stock Exchange. The New Ways to Work local authority survey (1987) found that 11 per cent of the 2000 job sharers were working at senior officer level and above. There are now many examples of shared jobs at principal officer level and above (salary range £14,000–£22,000).

More recent examples within local authorities include an assistant housing services manager in Kensington and Chelsea responsible for 28 staff; a principal personnel officer; a principal accountant for the London Borough of Enfield; and a divisional occupational therapist for Gloucestershire County Council.

Sally Hogg and Helena Carey share the job of manager in charge of 75 staff in the central Bristol child and family resource team. They comment that cover for sickness or holiday was a problem before the job share started, whereas there is now cover for three days a week. They emphasise that each of them trusts the other's professional ability, has confidence in her judgements and has a ready-made consultant when problems arise.

Assistant Chief Housing Officer, Colchester Borough Council

This £18,000 a year job, with responsibility for more than 70 staff, has been shared since March 1988; Gill Lewis had worked in the post full time for three years. Her initial application to the council to job share met with little support. After almost a year of negotiation and persuasion, her employer eventually agreed to advertise for a job-share partner and Mary Griffiths was appointed.

Gill works the first two and a half days of each week and Mary the second two and a half days. They usually arrange to have an overlap of about an hour on Wednesday lunchtime, when one hands over to the other. When for some reason they cannot meet, they have left each other notes, recorded messages on a dictaphone, telephoned each other at home, or delivered messages and pieces of work to each other's home. The key elements in this relationship have been sharing information and building a relationship of mutual trust.

Over the months Mary and Gill have evolved a system whereby each partner leaves the other a list of jobs outstanding, with suggested priorities, so they both know what needs to be done next. They tried initially to work with two diaries and two sets of in-trays, so that each partner could be responsible for one piece of work. They very soon found it better to share all tasks. Whoever is working on any particular day now accepts responsibility for continuing with whatever tasks have been started by her partner. This type of working has proved very fruitful, as a fresh eye on a half-finished task is often just what is needed to clarify a problem.

The job involves supervision of about 37 office-based staff, plus 28 wardens and care assistants based on estates throughout the borough. Mary and Gill decided not to supervise, say, half the staff each, because this would mean that on days when 'their' manager was not working, half the staff might feel they had no immediate contact point. They emphasise that this chosen pattern of working depends on the co-operation and support of their colleagues. It means that team meetings for one section of staff can no longer always be on a Thursday afternoon, for example: one week the meeting has to be in the first half of the week, and one week in the second half, to allow both job sharers to remain involved.

In projects involving external agencies, it has been more difficult to avoid specialism. Certain joint meetings with the health authority always take place on Fridays, so it is always Mary who attends. However, back in the office, they try to overcome this polarisation: for instance, Gill may do the preparation or follow-up work for the meeting that Mary attends.

Mary and Gill were aware that in sharing supervision of staff, there might be a danger that one of them would be played off against the other. They have never found this to be a problem in practice. Their boss's view is that he had to be talked into agreeing job sharing in the first place, and did have some doubts about it. He now admits to having been pleasantly surprised. The view of more junior staff is that it has made unexpectedly little difference to their lives.

Principal Social Worker, Sheffield City Council

Linda Gregory describes how she and John Randall shared this post:

'We're responsible for ten members of staff. We've split the team so that we have set people we supervise. It's been quite difficult to do it any way that clearly makes sense, but we have specialised slightly according to interests. There are problems, in that you're not around for people sometimes, but at least someone is there. I think very occasionally we lose something between meetings, but no more than a full-timer; there are different pressures for a full-timer. We both usually go to team meetings.

'Our direct line manager is the Divisional Officer, and he offers individual supervision sessions. We also have management team meetings of some sort every week. Wednesday mornings are completely taken up with meetings, and we alternate those. The divisional management team have been quite positive – they feel that we offer different areas of skill, and they've been very supportive.

'Occasionally you can't follow things through, and I sometimes find that quite frustrating. On the positive side, it's a very pressurised area we work in, it's very busy and we're under-staffed and under-resourced. It is quite tiring and demanding, so doing half a week is quite a relief.'

When the job share was reviewed by the team members, the main frustration expressed was the difficulty of arranging important meetings. No one felt they couldn't cope with the job share and it was acknowledged that there is a value in having two people do the job as it is so pressurised.

Within the Health Service, there is a range of shared higher level managerial posts. They include consultant psychiatrists in Bristol and principal pharmacists for Parkside Health Authority.

Dr Jane Maxim and Dr Sheila Wurtz share the job of co-ordinator of the BSc degree at the College of Speech Scientists. They are in charge of 200 undergraduates, teaching, taking part in clinical work and doing research.

A Chief Speech Therapist post was detailed as one of the case studies in the IMS report, *Job-Sharing in the National Health Service*. As a head of a small department there is a significant managerial component to the job. They tend to think along the same lines, and agree sufficiently on matters of clinical judgement as well as on managerial issues for each to be able to support decisions the other has made.

Managing staff seems to work well, and the view of subordinates is that the two sharers 'do not disagree'. They have an implicit understanding not to contradict each other on managerial questions, and differences of emphasis are dealt with by qualifying what the other has said or done with 'riders', rather than disagreeing outright.

Unit General Manager, Camberwell Health Authority
Sue Osborn and Susan Williams share this £30,000 job. They control

a budget of £15 million. They had both worked in the NHS for about eight years. The two women have the same basic skills, but different personal qualities. One works all day Monday and Tuesday, afternoons Wednesday and Thursday. The other is in every morning and the whole of Friday. It's a high stress job, but they find they are capable of tackling much more in the time available, because they are more relaxed. They feel that their job share succeeds because they trust each other's judgement.

The private sector
Within the private sector there are growing numbers of shared managerial level jobs. These include a senior manager for British Telecom International and a branch manager for the Halifax Building Society.

Carol Wheeler and Sue Tumelty spent a year lobbying Air Call Communications Bristol branch before they were allowed to share the post of branch manager. They work from Wednesday to Wednesday and are on call alternate weekends. They even have a company car each by running two Ford Fiestas instead of the large saloon that goes with the job.

Brenda Livingstone and Rita Woodman have shared the job of manager of Health Plus, a mail order vitamin and mineral pill company. The secret of their success is, they believe, the fact that they never compete with each other. They are now responsible for 12 workers.

In mid-1989 Denise Laurent and Michele Marchant became job sharing managers at a Boots store in Bromley. Their job is that of beauty sales manager and they are responsible for a staff of 30.

Chapter 4

Getting a Shared Job

Would job sharing work for you?

You may be working full time and for whatever reason looking for a reduction in working hours. Alternatively, you may not currently have a job and are wanting to return on a less than full-time basis. Whatever your situation, you need to consider thoroughly:

- Can you afford to work less than full time?
- Would sharing a job suit your personality?

Can you afford it?

When calculating your take-home pay for working half time you will find that this will be slightly more than half your current full-time take-home pay, as the proportion of tax-free pay will be greater.

If you are sharing a job with your husband/wife, you will pay a lot less tax than if one of you is working full time, as you will both receive the basic tax-free allowance.

If you are not working but are receiving some form of state benefit as a single person or a single parent, you will need to work out how much you can earn without making yourself worse off by job sharing. If you receive a disability benefit, you should check how this will be affected.

Will it suit you?

Sharing a job involves a particular way of working which may not suit everybody. If you are thinking of reducing your working hours in some way and job sharing is one of the options, then it is important that you take a careful look at how you feel about your job, and the ways in which you like to work. You will need to consider the following points:

- Are you generally happy with your current job? If not (but you still want to job share), then it will be better to look for another job to share. If you feel negative about the job you already have, then sharing it will not solve the basic problems.

However, if you are essentially happy with the job, but feel that sharing it would ease the stress and pressure and give you time for other things, then carry on.

- Are you ready to give up part of your job? Some people identify very strongly with their jobs; they like to make decisions on their own and to be solely responsible for the outcomes. People who have transferred to job sharing from full-time work have found that it can be very difficult to release part of their responsibilities to someone else, particularly if they have been doing the job for a long time. You need to feel sure that you will be able to do this, while accepting that it may not be easy.

- Are your prepared to spend the necessary time, and do you have the determination, to convince your employers of the feasibility of sharing your job?

- Are you willing to spend time working out how the job can be shared, as well as to spend extra time and effort building a good working relationship with your job-sharing partner?

- Do you feel able to work as part of a team with your job-share partner? Job sharing depends on co-operation, not competition. You will be jointly responsible for carrying out the job; it will not work if you feel competitive towards your partner. One job sharer comments: 'Job sharing works by trust – if you have problems about accounting for work and time, job sharing accentuates them. You also have to have a sense of humour, supportive families and not be the sort of person who can't get on with someone else at their pace!'

- There can be some loss of job satisfaction, as tasks that you start off may be finished by someone else. Some sharers have found that this is in fact a bonus, whereas others find it difficult. A personnel officer commented that she did find it hard not to be there on the first day of someone she had interviewed.

- Time pressures can be difficult and sharers are frequently aware that they do put in extra time – but then, so do many full-timers.

If you are likely to be the only job sharers within an organisation or department, then you may find yourselves in a pioneering role. Also, full-time colleagues can feel jealous of the time you have away from work; they often forget that you also have less pay! It can take a while for the idea to become part of an organisation's culture. Judith Lathlean, in evaluating a shared ward sister's post, noted the resistance to change:

> 'Aggression and hostility seem to be an inevitable aspect of the implementation of change, especially where individuals feel threatened or vulnerable or seek stability. The introduction of job sharing was new and threatening and despite considerable plans and discussion still required time not only to be accepted but also welcomed.'

Sharing a job will not suit everybody. It is important to think through these points before committing yourself.

Finding a shared job

To a large extent, job sharing has been initiated by people already working for an employer full time; however, others have been successful when applying for full-time posts advertised as open for job-share applicants, either with or without a partner. As the idea has become more acceptable, persuading some employers has become easier. In fact, in some cases it has been the employer who has suggested the idea.

Jill Dodwell-Groves and Sue Stevens applied individually for a senior post in the personnel department in Camden in 1981 and had both said that they wanted to do it on a part-time basis:

> 'The thought of job sharing hadn't actually occurred to us – we leapt at the opportunity and felt a bit silly not to have thought about it ourselves.'

The biggest changes in this area over the last seven years have been the number of employers agreeing overall job-share schemes where all jobs are seen as potential job shares. Some local authorities give employees returning after maternity leave the right to return on a part-time or job-share basis.

Negotiating from full time

Probably the easiest way of organising a job share is if you can find someone else within your department at the same level who also wants to reduce their hours. If your employer has a job-share policy, getting this agreed should be fairly straightforward. However, it will still be important to:

- start the negotiations as far as possible ahead of when you want to start job sharing
- present a well thought-out document detailing how you think the job could be shared.

Sheila McPhee, unable to cope with full-time work as a senior manager for British Telecom after returning from maternity leave, researched the idea of job sharing with her colleague Ann when she became pregnant. They prepared a case to show how it would work for them. Then fearing rejection, they invited their boss out to lunch.

'He was very disconcerted by this invitation to lunch . . . but he reacted positively straight away . . . what a super idea! We'd got all these arguments ready and it was completely unnecessary. He said, "What a good idea, which job are you going to share?"'

Even if there is no one else wanting to share, if the employer has a job-share policy then it is usual for him to advertise for the other half. For some people this will be easier than for others. For example, if you have the right to return after maternity leave on a job-share basis, then there is usually a set procedure to be followed in terms of the amount of notice required. Leeds City Council, for example, require three months' notice before your return.

Although an employer may be keen to retain a member of staff, the idea of a particular job being shared may cause problems. Even where there is a policy, managers may have strong views about the level at which jobs can be shared. However, experience indicates that it is worth being persistent. It took Jill Lewis almost a year of negotiation before her employer would agree to advertise for a partner (see Chapter 3 for details and more examples of higher level jobs which have been successfully shared).

Even if your employer won't agree to a job share, it may be possible to obtain agreement to reduce your hours while remaining at the same level. Although this may not be your first choice, it may be the best option at the time.

Philippa worked for a borough which did not have a job-share policy and wanted to share her job after maternity leave.

'Following the refusal of my job-share request in 1988, I was told that I already had a job to which I was entitled to return following maternity leave – a full-time one. My options were to work full time or resign. To cut a very long story short, I did not let the matter drop and, after advice from the Equal Opportunities Commission regarding possible sex discrimination and a possible industrial tribunal case, I was offered a newly created part-time post in a different section on the same grade, which I accepted. At present in my authority I am the only professional officer not working full time and other problems regarding conditions of service etc have since arisen.'

Your employers may not have a policy, but if they are keen to keep you then they may be willing to consider a job share. It can take a while to organise, and a lot of work, but it is worth persevering.

Frances Wheat had been working for Westminster City Council for six years before taking maternity leave in 1983. She then decided that she wanted to work part time, which her chief officer and the rest of her team accepted in principle. Job sharing was not seriously considered at that time because a previous job share had not been entirely successful. However, the personnel department objected to a supervisor working part time, saying that it was acceptable up to the level of senior officer, but not for a principal officer. They therefore suggested she be downgraded to senior officer. Both management and unions objected to this, as it would have meant Frances doing the same job for less pay, squashed into half the hours. Personnel then suggested a job share. Frances contacted New Ways to Work and within a week had put together a package on how the job share would work. This was presented to the departmental management. Initially they were split down the middle, but eventually they agreed.

Applying for a job-share post

It is now possible to find a range of job-share posts advertised, particularly with local authorities and in the voluntary sector. Health authorities are increasingly likely to advertise in this way too. It is worth looking at the appointments pages in the major newspapers; job-share posts are regularly advertised in the public appointments pages of the *Guardian*, in particular (see Chapter 7 for examples of adverts).

The selection process should be as in any other job, but in many cases you will be given the opportunity to meet the person already in post informally.

Applying with a partner

1. *For a job which is not advertised as open to job-share applicants*

In this situation it is very likely that an employer will not have thought of job sharing before, or even know what it is. It is thus very important to make a strong case for yourselves. In addition to working out the details set out on page 46, it will also be a good idea to include some information on what job sharing is and the practicalities involved when employing job sharers. You could include a copy of New Ways to Work's short fact sheet, 'Job sharing: an introduction for employers'. Alternatively, you could write your own version of this, using the information given in Chapter 7.

Frances Wheat, successful in obtaining two job-share posts with local authorities who did not at the time have job share policies, suggests:

> 'There are clearly many real benefits to employers if they can in the first place be persuaded to give job sharing a try. To this end it does seem worthwhile, if an employer doesn't have a policy, to present a carefully worked out package and market it, if necessary spoon-feeding the technical/administrative arrangements.'

Even if an employer is not open to the idea of job sharing to begin with it is worth being persistent, as was the case with the following people.

Geoff and Laura saw a job advertised with an independent research organisation which they were interested in applying for. When they rang up, they were told that job-share applications would not be considered. After further thought they rang again and following some discussion were told they could apply together, but 'you'll have to convince us'. They obviously did, because after two interviews, and out of about 70 applicants, they were offered the job together (see page 48 for the joint covering letter which they sent with their application).

2. *For a job with an employer who has a job-share policy*

Where an advert states that the job is open to job-share applicants, it may or may not make it clear whether you have to apply with a partner. Here are some examples:

> **JOB SHARERS WELCOME**
>
> **OPEN TO JOB-SHARE APPLICANTS**

In these cases, it isn't clear whether you need to apply with a partner, so you would have to check up. Other employers do make it clear:

JOB SHARERS WELCOME, WITH OR WITHOUT PARTNERS

JOB SHARERS MAY APPLY WITH A PARTNER

For your part, if you are only willing to be considered with the partner you apply with, you should make this clear. It is important you discuss with your partner what you will do if, after interview, only one of you is offered the job – with another partner. It is vital to agree on this. You may both feel that it is very important for you to share a job together, and that it is more important than one of you getting a particular job. This can create a difficult situation, especially if you are applying with a friend or relative.

In one situation where this happened, the person who was being offered the job with another partner was given the opportunity to meet the new partner. She did this, and having discussed it with the person she originally applied with, decided to take the job.

A number of the local authority schemes assess joint applications by first assessing you with the partner you have applied with and second with each and every other person who has applied to job share. Camden Council's guidelines state that:

> 'Interviewers are perfectly entitled to make any selection according to assessed ability: for example to appoint: an applicant for full time; a joint job-share application; to appoint one half only of a joint job-share application either with another individual job-share applicant or with no other appointment, and then to advertise the other half.'

Applying alone for a full-time job which welcomes job-share applicants with or without a partner

Many employers will not consider you unless you apply with a partner. However, some local authorities consider job-share applicants singly and, if they are the 'best person for the job' and there are no other suitable job-share applicants, will appoint them on their own and then advertise for the other half. Ines Newman applied for the job of Principal Economic Development Officer for Harlow District Council and was interviewed alongside full-time applicants. She was appointed as a job sharer and Harlow advertised for a partner; after two advertisements they were successful in finding a suitable candidate.

Finding a partner

1. *If you are already in a job* and want to job share in order to move into another one, perhaps at a higher level or in a different department, then it is worth asking around among colleagues. In particular, try approaching any women who are about to take maternity leave, or anyone you are aware of who has outside interests or other responsibilities.

Maureen Pascoe and Barbara Sorby were both part-time library assistants, working at the lowest clerical grades. They met at a staff party and discovered they were both in the same position. They were also, by coincidence, both about to start on a one-day-a-week degree course in librarianship. However, they realised that even when they got their degrees there weren't any professional opportunities for part-timers. They then came up with the idea of job sharing. It took them months of unsuccessful applications before they were accepted as job sharers for a Senior Library Assistant's post. During this period, they got to know each other very well and learnt to work together in the process. Years later, they were jointly promoted to Central Children's Librarian.

Carolyn Altounyan and Angela Probart sat opposite each other in their jobs as personnel officers. When they both became pregnant, the idea of job sharing together cropped up in conversation. Their employer had a job-share policy and they started sharing when Carolyn returned from maternity leave.

In another case it was almost by chance that a woman working as a draughtsperson ended up job sharing. She explains:

> 'I gave in my notice as full time was becoming difficult. I was asked to stay extra time so that they could have a new person working before I left. However, I met someone in a different department doing the same sort of job; we thought of job sharing, I suggested it to the departmental manager and it was accepted.'

The employer involved did not have a policy on job sharing, but as it is difficult to recruit skilled staff in this area, the firm was obviously very pleased to retain someone who "'as otherwise about to leave.

2. *Ask around generally* among friends and contacts. Make sure everyone you know is aware that you are looking for a partner. There are examples of jobs shared by husband and wife, sisters and brothers.

3. *You could advertise in a professional journal*, local paper or union newspaper. The *Library Association Journal* at one time had a job-sharing column in its vacancies section.

4. *Apply to one of the job-share partner registers*, which aim to match you up with others looking for a similar type of job. New Ways to Work runs a computerised register for the London area, and Sheffield Careers Office operates one for the Sheffield area.

Mary Kidston and Shirley Karat met through the NWW register in 1982. Mary, a town planner with ten years' experience but out of work when she registered with New Ways to Work, was contacted by Shirley, also a qualified town planner. Shirley had continued to work on a freelance basis for the consultancy firm she had been with for two years following the birth of her daughter. However, the work was erratic and she was paid on a part-time hourly rate. Wanting to get her hours on a regular footing and seeing Mary's details on the register, Shirley wrote to her; they met and found they got on well.

For Judith, the fact that she had added her name to the Sheffield Job-Share Register meant an opportunity to apply for a job which she had missed out on when it was first advertised, although she had been looking for a job share for about a year. The person who was appointed turned the job down. Someone from the organisation then looked at the register, which is on open access in the Careers Library in Sheffield, and contacted her, asking if she was interested in applying. She applied, was interviewed and appointed.

5. *Contact your professional body or trade union*. A number of these now have registers which aim to match you up with a partner, for example the British Medical Association, the Royal Town Planning Institute (see Appendix 2).

6. *Approach local employment agencies*. There are a number which specialise in job sharing (see Appendix 2).

Gemini, launched in February 1986, is a commercially run recruitment agency, based in Chelmsford, specialising in job sharing.

Even if an agency does not specify job sharing, you can sell yourselves together. Two women in south London were successful in doing this as early as 1980. They applied together for temporary summer work as job sharers, and after a while they were appointed permanently, working the same arrangement, to a firm in the City.

7. *Contact the organisations listed below*, who may have groups in your area. Go to a meeting or contact your local group explaining that you are looking for a job-share partner (see Appendix 2 for addresses).

Women and Training Group
Working Mothers Association
Women Returners Network

Applying for a job

Preparing together

Once you have found a partner you will need to spend some time getting to know each other. You should both list your particular skills, qualifications and experience. Look at:

- strengths
- weaknesses
- preferences.

If you do this now, you will be able to refer to it each time you apply for a job. It is important to recognise that, as with any search for a full-time job, you may have to apply for a number of jobs before you are successful. It can be a real advantage to have the support of another person in your search for a job, as you will be able to divide the tasks involved, such as scanning newspapers, between you. You will also have the support of another person to keep you going during the job search.

While Mary Kidston and Shirley Karat were looking together for jobs they met frequently and discussed how they would sell themselves as job sharers to an employer. They sent two curricula vitae and a joint covering letter with each application. They stress the importance of making out a convincing case to prospective employers:

'You've got to be serious about working out the application, and get across the point about being able to offer a wide range of experience.'

Eventually their hard work paid off. After ten letters and three interviews, they were offered a one-year contract job with the Royal Town Planning Institute's Planning Aid for Londoners. It was a success, their employers were happy, and when the contract was almost up they applied together for another job. This was as a senior planning officer for the London Borough of Camden, which already had a job-sharing policy: again they were successful. After working there for three months they applied jointly for internal vacancies. They were delighted to find that Camden were not only prepared to employ job sharers but to allow their careers to develop and offer them management responsibility. The department recognised them as a well-integrated double act, offering good value for money, and promoted them to project officer on a Principal Officer grade.

Organising how you will share the job
In whatever way you are hoping to organise a job share you will need to work out how you will:

1. divide the responsibilities
2. organise a time schedule
3. communicate.

For examples of how job sharers organise these aspects, see Chapter 5.

1. Dividing the tasks and responsibilities
Start by looking at the original job description, and expand it with detail from your experience of the job if you have already been doing it full time. It is important that you divide the job so that you have equal shares of the interesting as well as the more routine parts. Although you may allocate a particular task to the partner who has done that type of work before, it can also be an opportunity for the other person to develop their experience. Bad feeling may develop if one person always gets the most interesting parts of the job.

2. Organising a time schedule
Jobs are shared in a wide variety of ways. Different divisions are to work half days, half weeks, alternate weeks, alternate fortnights, and even six months on, six months off. You will need to consider:

- The nature of the job
- Are there peak hours when it would be useful to have both sharers present?
- Is the work fairly routine and easy to get into? Some jobs, for example in research and policy, have a 'warm-up time' which means that it is more difficult to carry them out on a half-day basis whereas others, involving routine or even boring work, may be better carried out on a half-day arrangement.
- Your personal needs.

3. Communicating

You will need to be able to communicate effectively between yourselves, as well as with colleagues, superiors and possibly with those you are responsible for supervising.

It is the communication between you and your partner and the joint responsibility for the whole job which differentiates job sharing as a way of working from part-time work in general.

In 'Does Job Sharing Work?' (Industrial Society, 1988) communication emerged as the key issue in the detailed study of seven job shares. One manager commented that without effective communication, job sharing simply becomes 'two part-time jobs back to back'.

What systems will you use? The systems you develop for communication will depend on the nature of the job and the way in which you organise the sharing of tasks and time.

Job sharing does involve extra work in organising an efficient communication system and for many sharers it can mean confronting existing office systems which do not generally work very well. Although this could be stressful in the short term, it can lead to overall increased efficiency in an office.

Where there is supervision of others, it is particularly important for the communication system to be watertight (see Chapter 5).

Will there be an overlap period? This will depend very much on the nature of the job. In more routine jobs, there may be no need actually to meet. One woman who had job shared in a bank for years never met her partner, as they left each other notes. However, with most jobs an overlap period will be important. The extent to which this is appreciated by employers will vary. It will depend on whether they see it as a positive period, where ideas and information can be exchanged and there can be true use of the often-quoted bonus of job sharers: 'Two heads are better than one.'

Putting together a joint application

It is usual for each person to fill in a separate application form and to enclose a joint covering letter explaining how the job share would work and the advantages of having job sharers in the post. The application form is a good test of whether you can work well together. Although it can be supportive having another person to apply with, it can also be daunting as one sharer explains:

'Although you have the support of another person, you have the added responsibility that if your application is no good, you're letting the other person down. There is also a feeling that your application has to be twice as good as anyone else's, to get over the extra hurdle of job sharing. I think our obsession with application forms paid off, as were interviewed for every job for which we applied.'

Geoff and Laura sent the following covering letter when they applied together for a senior job with an independent research organisation, who had originally said they were not open to job-share applications. They got the job out of about 70 applicants.

Dear

Project Co-ordinators

Enclosed are our individual applications for this post. However, we would strongly prefer to be considered as a job-share partnership. We recognise that the organisation may have reservations about considering the job as suitable for sharing. We have therefore written a joint statement in which we set out the advantages of appointing us together and, as far as possible at this stage, how we would tackle the task.

We hope and trust that you will be sufficiently interested in the potential of our job-share partnership to offer us an interview at which the issues can be discussed.

Yours sincerely,

Project Co-ordinators

Statement in support of the job-share application

We believe that as a job-share partnership we would bring a greater, more varied and complementary range of skills and experience to the post than would an individual. While we recognise that the early, developmental phases of the work may at first sight seem less amenable to a job share, we believe that we have a strategy to deal with the possible difficulties. Further, we think that the particular advantages of our job-share partnership apply at the planning stage as well as at the implementation and project management stages.

Our separate applications demonstrate the particular skills and work experience that we each have. In a partnership these will complement one another. All are relevant to what will undoubtedly be a complex task requiring a variety of responses. Geoff, for example, brings skills in project management, administration, budgeting and financial control; staff supervision, management and co-ordination. Laura's skills include counselling, casework, advice work and work with volunteers.

From the beginning it would be possible to divide the work and allocate responsibility between us for investigation, consultation and assessment. While our aim would be to work two and a half days per week each, or two days in one week and three days the next, we would wish to be flexible in our approach. In some cases, it may be appropriate for us to make the contacts together. Examples would be a small number of individuals with particularly significant experience and/or with whom we would expect to work closely in the future; the handful of existing projects; meetings where two people can absorb and recall more than one. In such cases we would be prepared to arrange to work together.

In other cases, we would divide the individuals, organisations and departments to be contacted between us as appropriate – perhaps by local authority, or by relationship to the type of support service being planned. Collating and assessing the information would, we think, be positively enhanced by the fact that there would be two of us doing it. It is easy for an individual to be overwhelmed by a mass of distressing data and by the almost infinite needs of seriously disadvantaged people. Job sharing would not only help to counteract this, but, as two heads are better than one, would stimulate better, more creative decision making and planning.

Clarity in planning and dividing the tasks, plus thorough recording and communication would of course be essential. We are confident that we could do this well. We share a common perspective based on similar backgrounds in social work, community work and community development, with experience of working with people from different ethnic groups, and of developing projects. In order to facilitate communication, the sharing of information and the assessment work in general, we would wish to overlap for part of the week, perhaps for a half or full day. Flexibility would be the keynote.

Our personal reasons for wishing to job share are so that we can share the responsibilities of childcare; our professional reasons are that, especially given the complexity, stress and isolation of this post, we believe that together as two part-timers we can be more productive than one full-timer, while staying fresh, energetic and creative for longer.

Much of this statement has dealt with the initial stages of the job. It is, however, broadly applicable to the later stages when we would operate our job-share partnership in a similar way. It is worth noting that as job sharers we could provide double cover, for example at busy times, at complex meetings or when two meetings occur simultaneously.

Finally, if the organisation is concerned about the implications of employing job sharers for National Insurance and super-annuation payments, sickness benefit, employment contracts, etc, may we reassure you that any fears are groundless. We have some answers ourselves and are confident that further reference to such organisations as New Ways to Work and the Hackney Job Share Project will provide all the necessary information.

Joint applicants

Prepare thoroughly for the interview. It could be helpful to have a practice interview. You could ask a friend or relative to play the role of interviewer, so that you can practise answering as a team. One couple who wanted to share a job and childcare of their daughter were successful in obtaining a job share after four interviews together. In all cases, the employers were not anticipating or prepared for job-share applicants, and didn't quite know what to do with them. Sue Oppenheimer explains more fully in 'The experience of a would-be-job sharer', produced by Hackney Job Share in 1984.

'Each time we were given a joint interview – some of them gave us a little longer than they had done for other applicants – but none had thought to interview us separately, and we did not feel in a position to suggest this . . . The joint interview situation had many problems. It made us feel very unsure – each time a question was asked neither the interviewers nor us were sure who should answer it. Carlos and I were torn between not knowing whether the other would answer better or worse. It was impossible for us not to feel in competition, and our trust for each another was put to the test. All this over and above the feelings one normally experiences in an interview situation.

Finally, we were aware in each interview of a resistance to the idea of job sharing. It all made it much tougher than I had anticipated. We were unable to overcome these problems in the first two interviews and I came away feeling despondent and demoralised. In the face of those feelings of competition I had felt unsure and unable to push myself, and very inadequate in relation to Carlos – I felt it was my fault that we hadn't got the jobs. I felt we were trying to achieve the impossible, and I was very reluctant to apply for any more jobs and put myself on the line again.

Looking back on it, I suppose those interviews gave us the experience which finally made us successful. They made us realise that our mistake had been not to discuss and share enough beforehand. Only if we could trust each other, were clear about each other's ideas, strengths and weaknessess, could we present a coherent and confident image. This would break down the competition between us, and minimise our individual feelings of inadequacy. Instead of feeling, 'Oh dear, he knows about that and I don't,' I realised I could be aware that this was his strength and I had other strengths. It clarified who should answer which question too. In fact, contrary to my original fears, close discussion between us enabled us to express our individuality better . . .

The day before the third interview, Carlos and I spent a lot of time discussing the issues and politics involved. We went through the job description thoroughly, identifying our individual and joint skills, and thinking about how we could share the job. At the interview, all the candidates were brought together to discuss certain issues put to us. Carlos and I were at an immediate advantage because of the work we had done the previous day. This boosted our confidence. Later, in our own interview, we were much more in tune with each other than we had been at previous interviews.'

Carlos and Sue received a phone call the next day to be told that they were the best applicants for the job, but that the employer was very worried about the job sharing. They were asked to go in and discuss it further. Although this was not an entirely positive experience (one person was particularly opposed to their application), they did eventually get the job.

In the case of joint applicants, you will already know each other well from the preparation involved in applying for the job together. However, the interview situation is different and, as indicated above, you will need to sort out who is going to answer which questions. Employers who have never considered job share applicants before may not be sure how to interview you. It can help your preparation if you telephone beforehand and ask how you will be interviewed. Usual good practice is to interview you both separately and together. If you are each being interviewed separately on your ability to do the job, the joint part of the interview should concentrate on how you will do the job together.

You should make a list of the sort of questions likely to be asked and decide who will answer which. Some job sharers are only interviewed together, and in this situation it is important for you to be very clear about the points you want to get over.

During the interview, bear in mind two particular points:

1. Make your references to the benefits of job sharing very specific to this particular post and organisation. You will need to show that you have thought carefully about these points.

2. If the interviewers bring up problem areas to do with job sharing, try to think whether these problems relate to full-timers too. For example, a commonly expressed problem is what happens if the one of you involved in a case is not there when someone rings up? You can make the point that even full-timers are not there all the time – they are out at meetings, on holiday, etc. You should also explain how you will deal with this aspect.

Some questions you should be prepared for:

- *What is job sharing and why is it different from part-time work?* See Chapter 2.

- *What other employers use job sharing?* (Chapter 6). If the employer does not have any previous experience of job sharing, it is helpful to be able to give examples of jobs which are shared within your particular job type. If you can't find any references within this book then contact New Ways to Work, who may be able to put you in touch with someone. It is worth putting some effort into finding similar examples within the same type of organisation. For example, if you are applying for a job share in the retail sector it will carry more weight if you are able to give examples of how managers for the Boots Company are already sharing jobs, rather than the fact that teachers are sharing a job in the school down the road.

- *What are the main advantages to this organisation?* This is an opportunity to elaborate further on those benefits which you will already have outlined in your application. These can be related both to your specific partnership, eg the range of skills offered, and more general points such as the ability to attend two meetings at the same time, etc. Take some time going through the points listed on page 76 and think of the relevance to this job.

- *What are the costs?* Although you will need to acknowledge that there are extra costs in administration and training, you can emphasise the fact that benefits such as wages, holidays etc will be pro-rated.

- *What do I do if one of you leaves?* You can explain that the usual practice is for the employer to advertise the half post (see Chapter 7).

- *Why do you want to work part time?* If you are interviewed for a job in a local authority with a positive policy towards job sharing, you may not be asked this question. However, if you are asked, try to answer honestly and briefly, and emphasise that you are committed to continuing or returning to the work-force using the skills you have, and how this fits in with your long-term career plans. The stereotype of the part-time worker as uncommitted and only in it for pin money still remains in some employers' heads. If you are already working for the organisation, stress your desire to remain with it during this period of your life when you wish to reduce your hours, but not your commitment. An employer will need to be reassured that your desire to work on a less than full-time basis will not affect your ability to carry out the job.

Applying alone

These were some of the questions asked at interview where half a post was being filled.

'Are you able and prepared to:

- co-ordinate your hours of work to cover the week adequately and to overlap with your sharer once a week?
- receive telephone calls at home, if necessary?
- in exceptional circumstances vary your hours to cover important meetings?
- work closely with your job sharer on day-to-day organisation and overall approach?'

A potential job sharer explains her harrowing experiences of being interviewed for a head of department teaching post in 1983.

'We were interviewed together, and were the first to be interviewed, but there was a long delay of 20 minutes before we were called in. When we went in, the Chair of the panel said that a letter had been received from the education authority saying that if they should favour us as the ones for the job, the authority was not sure that we could be appointed as no proper agreement had yet been worked out.'

The interview got totally bogged down in details about how they would share the job, and never progressed to talking about their combined vast experience as teachers. The panel made an internal appointment of a full-time male teacher, with only three years' experience.

At the other extreme, two people who had been job sharing together for a number of years were interviewed together for a promotion. No questions were asked about how they would organise the job-sharing aspect – they had clearly already convinced the employer of that. They got the job!

After the interview

If you didn't get the job, it will be useful for future interviews to sit down fairly soon afterwards and discuss areas where you felt you didn't respond well, questions you did answer well, questions you weren't prepared for and any aspects you need more information on.

If you are a full-time employee whose job-sharing request has been turned down, you will need to consider your next step. If the organisation already has a job-share policy, then you should refer to any policy document or guidelines. Most have some form of grievance or appeals procedure which will allow your request to be reconsidered by a panel or some other forum (see page 116). Don't give up straight away: ask for the reasons why your request is not being considered.

Chapter 5

Making a Job Share Work

Getting started

In the first few weeks, it will be important to meet regularly and set up your systems. If you are both new to the job, then communication is a vital element of getting the job share off to a good start. In any new job, the first few months are in some ways a trial period; in a job share, this applies not only to you and your partner, but also to job sharing as a concept.

Even if you know your partner and have just been through the process of applying for jobs together, the beginning of the job share is a fresh start. If one of you was previously doing the job full time it is especially important that you are both aware of the potential difficulties of this situation. Set a date to review how things are working.

Remember, the key words are co-operation and communication. Some job sharers actually arrange to work together for the first few weeks, and some employers arrange for you both to attend any induction training. The Boots guidelines for managers state that new partners should go through the induction programme together. This saves time and also allows a relationship to be established.

In their study of 'Job Sharing in South-East Essex' in 1986 Patricia Leighton and Catherine Rayner concluded that there were two types of job share. The first, which they termed the 'integration model', 'sees the partners taking more or less joint responsibility for the job tasks and decision making. Such an arrangement clearly requires efficient communications systems and high levels of trust. It also requires that careful consideration be given to the management of job shares.'

For the second model, they note that 'for many people in employment, job sharing can simply connote a more refined and secure form of part-time work. The hours of the full-time post are divided, but the degree of joint responsibility and interchangeability as between the partners is at a lower level than in the "integration model". However, there may be better communication than between ordinary part-timers, and they may well be more absorbed into the structures and administration of the enterprise. We called the second form of job sharing the "demarcation model".'

In Mary Pritchard's study, over half the sharers said that the job was divided by a combination of time and task/project/client basis. The second most common arrangement (36 per cent) was by time only.

Schedules

Even if you worked out a schedule when you were applying for the job, it may be necessary to modify it once you know when regular meetings are held. Some of the questions you will need to consider are listed below. If any have already been fixed and agreed at interview, start with them:

1. *How much time can/should be spent together?* In the Industrial Society study 'Does Job Sharing Work?', the researchers concluded that the most successful job shares in their judgement tended to be those where sharers had greater contact with each other and the work could be more coherent and cohesive.

2. *Are there meetings at which both need to be present?*

3. *Are there times when you could both attend two different events at the same time?*

4. *Is it necessary to have nine-to-five cover every day of the week?* Is it possible to use the flexitime system to provide cover during core times, but still allow for a reasonable overlap? It is important to remember that full-timers are not there all the time. If there is a time of week – say Friday afternoons – when work is slacker, than it may be feasible for neither to be present.

One set of sharers whose job does not need them to cover the office from nine to five every day organise an overlap by each working three days a week. They 'clock up' approximately six hours a day and cover core time within the organisation's flexitime scheme. One does Monday, Wednesday and Friday, the other Tuesday, Thursday and Friday. They feel this gives full office cover, a reasonable spread of days and a full day's overlap for joint working on particular topics. Overlap time is difficult to arrange in teaching jobs, particularly in nursery and primary schools; sharers often have to meet during the lunch hour.

5. *Are there peaks and troughs in the work which need to be covered fairly?* In this context, would it be useful for sharers to work together at the peaks, and for the job not to be covered during the troughs? If this is not feasible, then it will be important to organise schedules so that one person does not always work at the busiest time of the week.

6. *How can any personal preferences be fitted into this?*

Examples of schedules

The split day
This provides a potential overlap every day, although this may not be necessary.

> Marcia and Andy shared a job as an instructor in a Social Services day centre, with Andy working in the morning and Marcia the afternoon. They met once weekly on a formal basis for half an hour, but informally every day to exchange information.
>
> 'At first we made the mistake of not jotting things down, and consequently our remembered reports of the morning's or afternoon's briefing and activities were often not complete. A notebook, pen and measure of resolve have overcome this problem. On average we report and chat for 20 minutes or so daily. I really do believe we have established one of the best working relationships in the building. It has also, I feel, by example enhanced the way other staff communicate between themselves.'

The split week
This can be organised as follows:

A works Monday to Wednesday lunchtime; B works Wednesday lunchtime to Friday. This gives the possibility of a small overlap of, say, an hour on Wednesday.

Another arrangement is for A to work Monday, Tuesday and alternate Wednesdays; B to do Thursdays, Fridays and alternate Wednesdays. This does not allow for an overlap within office hours. Also, you should be aware of employment protection aspects (see Chapter 8).

> Linda and John, senior social workers, work this arrangement, but because they live together, they are able to communicate at home! Team meetings are on a Monday morning and although

John does not work on a Monday, he does attend them. They last about one and a half hours and he takes time off in lieu.

Alternate weeks

Daphne and Freda shared a job as management secretary in a bank for many years. They worked alternate weeks, performing their duties as they arose during the week. They found that there was not a great deal to be carried over from one week to the next. So that they could quickly keep up to date with what had been going on in their absence, they kept an extra copy of all letters for each other to read on Monday mornings.

Where a job does not need 100 per cent coverage it is possible for both sharers to work, say, on a Friday morning to overlap and for there to be no coverage on a Friday afternoon.

A variation which is becoming more popular is for each sharer to work Thursday to Wednesday, or Wednesday to Tuesday. Although there is no overlap in this, again it can be built in, if total coverage is not needed.

Angela and Heidi found that the best way to share their ward sister's post was to work Wednesday to Wednesday, with an overlap period – often half a shift on a Wednesday.

Alternate days

A works Monday, Wednesday and Friday morning; B works Tuesday, Thursday and Friday afternoon, with an overlap on Friday lunchtime. This division of time is often popular where people divide projects or clients between them, for example social workers or health visitors.

Frances and Maggie are planners who take the 'lead' on different projects, but keep up to date with each other's work. They work alternate days so that there is never more than one day before the 'lead' on a particular project is in again.

There are also examples where people work two weeks on/off, a month on/off and six months on/off, where this suits the needs of the job and their own needs. These arrangements are, however, less common, and it is important to consider how benefits and pensions will be affected.

There is a whole range of variations on these basic schedules. For example:

Olive and Viv are GPs who divide surgery time between them by each working for one whole day and three half days a week, with one whole day off. They share the equivalent of a single full-time partner's on-call work, and alternate night duty, each doing one night every two weeks.

Dividing the tasks and responsibilities

The starting point for this is usually the job description. Each point can be considered and discussed in relation to whether tasks will be shared out or carried out by whoever is in. At this point, if you did not apply for the job together and have not already gone through the process outlined on pages 45–46, it will be helpful also to consider each person's preferences, strengths and weaknesses. For both sharers to feel that they are equal partners, it is essential that a fair division of tasks is agreed on: there may be certain tasks which are particularly popular and others which are not. It is important to be aware of this point when one person has been in the post previously.

In some jobs, tasks will be carried out by whoever is there: for example, sub-editors, typists, gardeners. In others, types of tasks are varied, and although some can be carried out by whoever is there, it may be necessary for the sharers to divide clients, projects or cases: for example social workers, landscape architects, health visitors. The extent to which sharers cover for each other when tasks are divided in this way varies. Two GPs have their own lists, although they occasionally see each other's patients.

The role of meetings within a department or section can be a very important part of the job. Where there are certain regular key policy meetings, it may be necessary for both sharers to be present; for other meetings this may not be necessary, and sharers may be able to take it in turns (although this can be difficult if meetings are always held on a particular day).

Communication and overlap

Where work is very self-contained, little or no communication may be needed, other than written notes to explain what point the work has reached. However, communication in many job shares is a vital ingredient.

Sharers facilitate communication in a variety of ways. Many

comment that because of the need to communicate effectively, they are better organised. In 'Does Job Sharing Work?', virtually everyone interviewed emphasised the extra responsibility that job sharing involves in terms of organising and communicating their own work. A few people also noted that efficient communication with sharers, as well as from them, requires examination of the systems currently in use.

Methods of communication usually include a combination of books, files, and phone calls at home. Gillian Lewis and her partner who share the post of Assistant Chief Housing Officer in Colchester, have left each other notes, messages recorded on a dictaphone, telephoned each other at home, or delivered messages and pieces of work to each other's homes. Sharers who do not regularly overlap in the office may ring each other at home at each changeover point. Bristol City Council will meet the extra costs of communicating, such as additional telephone charges.

> Nursing sisters Judith and Elizabeth overlap on a Wednesday for two hours to give time for mutual discussion, patient briefing, and to make contact with personnel contributing to the work in general, such as nursing tutors and medical company representatives. They find the overlap essential to ensure good continuity of care and communications. To aid this they keep a detailed 'Kardex' system on the patients, a diary and message book. They say that 'although this period of overlap to an employer may appear wasteful financially, we have found that working closely together has led to greater creativity, each of us stimulating the other. Through working less hours we have found in some ways we are more committed and productive in our work.'

One sharer illustrates how important it is to be clear not only on the form of communication, but the way it is carried out.

> 'Although we are alike in the most important ways, there are differences in "style", which can cause misunderstandings if we don't take care. For instance: the clear, detailed, and diplomatically worded notes we must write each other daily can become a time-consuming chore. When we write in haste, one of us tends to become confusingly verbose, the other succinct to the point of dropping an occasional key word. Sloppy handwriting is another occasional problem.'

Other considerations

Liaising with colleagues

Communication with colleagues, managers and staff being supervised is important, and again a variety of methods is used. Wall calendars can indicate when each person is in; some sharers put a notice on the door saying which days they will be working.

Where job sharers work as members of a team, it is essential to consider how the job share will affect other team members. You will need to work out systems of communication with other members, particularly where they are likely to have to take messages or cover for you. In 'Does Job Sharing Work?', colleagues of sharers sometimes discussed the additional communication burden this arrangement imposed upon them. The study concluded that it is vital to plan tasks, work time and cover and this is probably best dealt with in consultation with the whole work unit.

Social workers explain how they attempt to counter the criticism of part-timers that they are away from the office for long periods.

> 'We attempt to counter this by splitting the working week, with one of us working Monday and Thursday and the other working Tuesday and Friday. Wednesday we each work half day, alternating between mornings and afternoons so that we can attend Wednesday morning team meetings once a fortnight. Because of these arrangements, we feel confident that our colleagues never have to cover any work as a result of our job sharing, and we have never had any adverse reaction from clients.'

Attitudes of colleagues

It is clear from Mary Pritchard's research that organisations often view job sharing as having less status than full-time work. There is sometimes a feeling of resentment that, even though job sharing has been established for a number of years, sharers still had to be 'pioneers'. Many job sharers feel undervalued and that they have to be better than full-timers to prove themselves. One writes of the initial distrust and hostility; she finds that 'job sharing is seen as an easy get-out for part-timers.' Another wrote; 'Colleagues don't appreciate the organisation required.'

Male job sharers may meet extra prejudice because working part-time does not fit in with the stereotype of the male worker. For example, one man was told by a large commercial employer: 'We expect our employees to want to work overtime, not part time.'

Another male sharer said, 'Sometimes I feel a bit guilty, as though I have a soft option and I'm not always sure what my colleagues think.'

Working more than contractual hours

Sixty-five per cent of job sharers interviewed by Pritchard said that they regularly worked more than their contractual hours, and of these 30 per cent received no recognition of any sort for these extra hours. The most usual recognition was time off in lieu or flexitime (59 per cent).

Job sharers in the voluntary sector in particular frequently mention this as a problem:

'I found it quite difficult, in a job with flexible hours and never-ending amounts of work that could be done, not to do more than half time.'

Difficulties may arise where time off in lieu or flexitime are allowed, as it can be very difficult for sharers to arrange to take that time off. Of course, many full-timers work extra hours too, but that does not mean that this should be generally taken for granted.

Male/Female roles

A couple who shared the job of organiser at a community centre in Norfolk found that:

'Despite similar qualifications, many people see Alan as the main worker in control of the project. I'm seen in a supportive/secondary role.'

In another case, a husband and wife who share a university lecturer's job were given different job titles: he was a lecturer while she was an associate lecturer.

Different partners

Don MacDonald shared the job of Training Manager at the Stock Exchange for a number of years, with two partners. He found that it worked differently depending on the personalities and back-grounds involved. He and his first partner divided tasks more between them, whereas with his second partner he developed a different, more informal relationship 'tending to share individual projects as well as the job'.

Relating to people outside the organisation

People new to the idea of job sharing are often concerned about the effect two people sharing a job may have on outside clients and members of the public. There is sometimes a false assumption that full-timers are there all the time, which is clearly not the case: people take holidays, are ill and go to meetings. In the area of health care, people frequently have to relate to more than one person. As two sharers point out:

> 'We have found that people are not confused having two stoma care nurses to deal with – possibly due to the fact that they have to relate to many professionals, so this is just one more.'

Overcoming problems

The following case history of two people sharing the job of librarian contains some typical problems. One explains:

> 'I found it difficult at first to share a job with someone who had been doing this particular post full time for more than 12 years, and I think she must have experienced difficulties in reverse. We fortunately got on well together personally, which has helped the transition.
>
> The practical difficulties of managing a department which operates six days a week from 9 am to 9 pm and involves shift and rota working have been considerable. The need to communicate precisely and concisely on our respective decisions and ongoing projects has been highlighted and is inevitably time-consuming. An overlap period of half a day per week was aimed at to begin with, but has been difficult to maintain due to shift/rota requirements.
>
> After seven months, I think the job has tended to split into Ann (the original postholder) taking major responsibility for 'housekeeping' aspects, as she is still more familiar with procedures and stocktaking, whilst I have taken on some new project work. We both cope with day-to-day management and enquiry work as it crops up. "Personnel management" has also been quite difficult to organise, due to a combination of job share and shift/rotas making it difficult to meet with the staff regularly.
>
> We have also of course had to educate the other staff within the organisation on job sharing, ie that they do not need to

speak to both of us every time an issue occurs or that only one of us will attend a particular meeting (representing both sharers though). Arranging meetings and attending working parties is also difficult, as one of us may have been dealing with a particular topic but be unable to attend the relevant meeting.

Interestingly, we have so far seen only a very few examples of people trying to play one of us off against the other. For instance asking both of us for a decision and, where it has been different, choosing the one which suits the enquirer the best!

In conclusion I would say "the experiment continues" and is proving very interesting for both of us and hopefully not too traumatic for the other members of staff in the department.'

Chapter 6

Which Employers Take on Job Sharers?

The number of organisations employing job sharers has grown dramatically over the past five years. It is only within the last few years that surveys have even asked whether job sharers are employed.

An ACAS survey of 548 companies carried out in 1987 found that 10 per cent of respondents had introduced job sharing over the past three years and 7 per cent planned to introduce or increase it in the future. Its growth was greatest in industries which employ mainly white-collar staff, such as public administration and banking, where over a third had introduced it. The highest proportion of employers with job sharing was in the south east (16 per cent).

In an Equal Opportunities Commission survey of local authority equal opportunity policies in 1986 it was found that over one-third (179) of local authorities in Great Britain provided job-sharing opportunities for some of their staff.

In 1988, Part Time Careers Ltd, a recruitment agency based in central London, carried out a survey of 157 companies who had employed part-timers on a regular basis. They found that 23 per cent had employed two people 'twinned to share one full-time job'.

A Blue Arrow Personnel Services survey of 2,000 companies in 1989 revealed that 16 per cent operated job-share schemes, but only in a limited way; 38 per cent said they were prepared to consider job sharing, but only if pairs of sharers applied together. A more recent survey of 1000 personnel professionals, carried out by the Institute of Personnel Management in 1989, found that 25 per cent offered job sharing.

Pritchard found that 78 per cent of sharers interviewed were working in the public sector, 16 per cent in the voluntary sector and 6 per cent in the private sector. Well over half (57 per cent) worked in organisations with over 1,000 employees, and 25 per cent in organisations with 100 employees or less. Only 18 per cent worked in medium-sized organisations. A sizeable minority, (29 per cent) said they were the only job sharers in the organisation.

The private sector

In the past, a number of employers used a form of job sharing (often referred to as 'twinning') as a way of coping with staff shortages. Some of the clearing banks in particular used 'alternate-week workers'. An early example of a job share at a higher level in the private sector was the post of Senior Training Officer at the Stock Exchange, first shared in 1981.

A survey of company equal opportunities policies carried out by Labour Research in 1988 found that of the 21 companies who replied out of 60, only five (27 per cent) made job sharing available. Furthermore, only one of these, the National Westminster Bank, could state the number of employees in job shares. Here, two workers shared jobs in what the bank said was 'just being introduced as part of a career break scheme'. Other employers who said job sharing was available, British Telecom, British Gas, ICI and Lloyds, either did not know the numbers or did not monitor centrally.

In June 1989, Industrial Relations Services surveyed 18 schemes in the private sector. However, most of these were informal arrangements, seven of which had only one or two shared posts. A number of companies said they were reviewing the whole range of employees' working patterns or were considering an official job-share policy. Although a number of the banks and building societies were employing larger numbers of job sharers, these were mainly in clerical, cashier and secretarial posts. British Gas had ten shared posts, from clerical to higher management, the policy being to retain maternity leavers if possible.

The *Financial Times* signed an agreement on job sharing with the National Union of Journalists in 1987. This states that 'Any journalist may request either that the filling of an existing full-time vacancy, or his or her own job, be considered on a shared basis.' The first job share at the *Financial Times*, negotiated by a husband and wife, started in 1984. There are currently two other sets of sharers.

The first full schemes were announced by Boots Retail Division and British Telecom in late 1988. British Telecom had experimented with job sharing in the west of Scotland, where 25 posts have been shared, ranging from clerical to middle management. The Employee Services Manager commented: 'Some of the job sharers might otherwise have left the company and we are now able to retain them.' Although British Telecom have agreed a framework for the development of local job-sharing arrangements with the National Communications Union (NCU), schemes will be negotiated locally.

Boots

Boots Retail Division launched its job-share scheme in November 1988 with a circular and poster sent to all managers. By November 1989 there were 38 job sharers, all women, mainly in the south east. The jobs are shared in a variety of ways and include posts for pharmacists, sales managers and senior sales assistants.

Interest was first shown by store managers who wanted to be able to recruit and retain good supervisory staff. They were concerned at the numbers of staff with supervisory capabilities who were not able to fulfil their own personal need to work part-time hours without dropping back to a lower grade. Previously, no part-time work had been available above the grade of general assistant, and thus anyone wishing to return part time would have had to return on a lower grade. This represented a waste of training, but it was hard to create part-time posts at supervisory and management level because of the full-time cover needed.

In the non-pharmacy grade, job sharing is possible at senior assistant and supervisor level and above, and in the pharmacy grades at pharmacy manager level and above. As very few posts at this level are advertised externally, requests have been from internal applicants. At present the scheme operates only within Boots the Chemist, but it could be used as a model for other divisions.

Although job sharing is a fairly well-known term within the public sector, this is not the case in the private sector. Boots therefore produced a poster both to advertise the scheme and raise awareness within stores about what job share means. The text of the eye-catching poster, headed 'Two talented people: one "full-time" career' is as follows:

'We're aware that the needs of the people who work for us differ greatly.

Staff wishing to progress careers can equally feel a responsibility to commitments outside work – a family perhaps.

To meet these changing needs Boots is pioneering the widespread introduction of job sharing for Senior Assistant level, and above.

It's more than simply working part time. A full-time position will be shared equally between two people while retaining all managerial or supervisory responsibility.

To do this successfully requires individuals with the communication skills to build a sound partnership – working closely together following a single management direction and cohesive policies.

For us it's a way to retain and recruit good people, who may no longer wish to work full-time hours, or feel they have more to offer than they can at present.

For you it is the chance to continue or develop the career you've worked hard for.'

Advertisements for senior assistants, supervisors and sales managers include a paragraph on job sharing as follows:

'This may be a job-share opportunity, which provides the chance to work the hours that suit your commitments. Supervisory (or management) responsibility will be shared equally between two people – requiring strong communication skills and the ability to work closely with one another.'

Area offices operate job-share registers; these also contain details of any external applicants who have expressed interest in job sharing.

Benefits
Boots believes that because job sharers work at times to suit their own commitments, they give 100 per cent effort. Sharers who work three days help to cover extended trading hours without relief staff. By reducing turnover, the company can make savings on recruitment costs and on the training of new pharmacy managers.

Costs
The additional costs involved in employing two job sharers are considered to be minimal, particularly compared with the total payroll and with the cost of replacing staff who leave. Training costs are of course higher, as each sharer needs training.

Administration is not a problem, as Boots already have many part-time staff as well as people working on term-time and variable hours contracts.

When the policy was introduced, fears expressed by line managers had to be overcome. However, this was found to be a problem of the way people think, rather than the nature of job sharing itself. Now area managers are fully behind the scheme and there have been no negative comments from line managers.

The Halifax Building Society
In July 1989 the Halifax Building Society introduced a job-share scheme as one of three equal opportunities initiatives, including

re-entry and career break schemes. These measures were the outcome of a joint working party of the society's management and its staff association. A circular explaining the provisions of the agreement was issued to all staff. Job sharing had been used before in clerical jobs, but this was more in the nature of part-time working. Job sharing has now been extended to junior management level 9 and above. The new scheme follows a pilot scheme in which two women shared a departmental manager's job.

Other companies
In smaller companies, a formal scheme may not fit into the culture of the organisation, but some may be open to requests from existing members of staff. Individual arrangements within the private sector include: a manager of a chemist's shop; branch manager of the Bristol branch of Air Call Communications; a senior information scientist for a chemical company.

Many companies are currently considering more flexible working arrangements. Recent press reports have indicated that American Express are to introduce a range of options including job sharing, and Jaeger in Ipswich has announced that they will offer women the chance to job share.

The public sector

1. The Civil Service
The Civil Service has not had a tradition of part-time working and in the main, job sharing is not differentiated from part-time working. In 1985 the Cabinet Office issued a guidance document to government departments encouraging them to extend the scope of job sharing and part-time working. It followed recommendations from a joint union/management review group on equal opportunities for women in the Civil Service which aimed at enabling women and men 'to combine easily a full career with domestic responsibilities'.

By 1989 there were 3,500 people sharing jobs. The majority of these are in the Department of Health, the Department of Social Security, the Department of National Savings and the Department of Employment Group; most are at Administrative Officer, Executive Officer and Administrative Assistant level. There are, however, some examples of job sharers in management and supervisory posts.

The then Department of Health and Social Security (DHSS) first introduced job sharing in 1983 and opportunities for part-time working in 1985. There are now 6,000 people working part time and a further 500 job sharers. Since part-time work has been available, the number of part-timers has grown steadily, and the number of job sharers fallen slightly. Part-time staff have more choice over the number of hours they work: over 60 per cent work between 21 and 30 hours per week. The majority of part-timers are on the Administrative Assistant grade. Part-timers do have equal access to promotion. When applying for promotion, anyone may indicate that he or she wishes to be considered for the post on a part-time basis.

2. Local authorities

Local authorities pioneered the introduction of formal job-share policies in the early 1980s, largely as part of equal opportunities initiatives. Research carried out by the Equal Opportunities Commission in 1980 found two local authorities with job-share policies, but neither had drawn up a full scheme. By 1986 an EOC survey found that over one-third of local authorities provided job-sharing opportunities for some of their staff.

A more detailed survey of these authorities carried out by New Ways to Work in 1987 revealed that 38 authorities outside London had formally adopted policies on job sharing, and a further 36 employed some job sharers. In addition, 18 of the London boroughs had a formal policy. By 1987 over 2,000 people were sharing non-teaching jobs in 56 authorities. One of the Scottish Regions, Strathclyde, had 100 job sharers at the time of the survey and now has 488. Leicester City, with 48 sharers in 1987, now have 139 and in Birmingham City sharers grew from 76 in 1986 to over 400 in 1989.

During the last year, policies have been announced by a wide range of authorities, including Oxfordshire County, Worcester City, Darlington Borough, Humberside County, Southampton City. In the early stages, some authorities restricted job sharing to lower grades, but many have revised their scheme to cover all grades.

The types of local authority jobs shared are very wide ranging and include accountant, librarian, careers officer, environmental health officer, home help organiser, housing officer, museums education officer, personnel officer, planner, receptionist, secretary, social worker, solicitor, typist (see Chapter 3). Social Services and Libraries Departments often have a high proportion of the total job sharers within an authority.

Sheffield City Council

Sheffield City Council was one of the first councils in the country to agree a job-share policy in principle, in 1981. Formal agreements have since been signed with the union, NALGO, for officer posts, and with the manual unions. By November 1989 292 non-teaching jobs were shared. All applications to job share need NALGO approval and a checklist is filled in by local shop stewards.

The number of sharers has steadily increased over the years, in spite of the lack of general publicity for the scheme. There is no standard information available for potential sharers, other than the agreement itself, and only a small number of job adverts state that job-share applicants are welcome. The standard application form does, however, include a question asking if the candidate wishes to job share, and some departments give further information to their staff. A large proportion of job shares are found within four departments: Family and Community Services, Libraries, City Treasury and Education.

The vast majority of job shares in Family and Community Services are initiated by women returning from maternity leave, but they also include people in their 40s and early 50s; in addition, employees are considering it from the pre-retirement angle. There is one example of three people sharing two jobs as community workers within the department.

One of the first job shares within the council was agreed within the Libraries Department, and started in July 1982; the individuals concerned played a pioneering role in gaining acceptance for the idea. There are currently 29 posts shared; all maternity leavers in City Libraries are informed about job sharing, and an informal network exists within the department. The majority of management are positive, although there is some concern about saturation of job sharers at one public service point.

3. Local education authorities

In 1982, Sheffield Education Authority was one of the first to invite teachers to apply for job sharing, in response to the unemployment situation. The Inner London Education Authority (ILEA) introduced a full job-share scheme in 1986, following a successful pilot scheme involving 70 shared posts in 1984–85 (see Chapter 3).

Existing schemes are being studied in greater depth by June Smedley at Loughborough University (see p. 17). Few sharers in new schemes were in promoted posts, but where job sharing had been accepted practice for a few years, more posts of responsibility were shared. There are a number of head of department shares, a few deputy head shares and at least one possible head teacher share is under discussion.

4. Health authorities

Lothian Health Board introduced job sharing in 1970 and since 1975 have operated a scheme which allows two people to apply for any grade of medical post from house officer to consultant. At the time of the EOC survey in 1980, four registrar posts, five senior registrar posts and one consultant post were being shared. Doctors usually submit a joint application for a full-time appointment and are asked to agree to share all the duties of the post in a manner acceptable to them and their colleagues.

It is now government policy for the National Health Service to encourage more part-time arrangements, including job sharing, both to promote equal opportunities and to help solve skills shortages.

In early 1989, the Institute of Manpower Studies (IMS) carried out the first national survey of job-sharing practice in the National Health Service. They found that more than half (92) of the health authorities and boards in the UK who responded now make use of job sharing, and that this has increased rapidly in the last three years. They identified 355 job-share posts and feel that the overall total may be 500. Most of these posts were introduced in response to requests from employees, rather than as part of any management-initiated strategy. Only 8 per cent of those with job-share posts had any formal policy or guidelines for their implementation, although many managers recognised the need for these as job sharing becomes more widespread within the NHS.

Health authorities are beginning to advertise jobs 'welcoming job-share applicants' or stating that job-share arrangements will be considered. Recent advertisers have included Barnet, Basildon and Thurrock, City and Hackney, North Hertfordshire, Tower Hamlets. The 1989 Industrial Relations Services survey also gave details of job sharing in five health authorities: East Hertfordshire, East Suffolk, Lothian Health Board, North Bedfordshire and West Midlands. East Suffolk Health Authority (Community Nursing) employ five pairs of health visitors in shared posts.

In April 1989, Leeds Eastern Health Authority was one of the first in the country to introduce a formal job-share scheme in an attempt to recruit and retain employees within the National Health Service.

The voluntary sector

Some of the early examples of job sharing were in the voluntary sector. At the time of the EOC survey in 1980, six of the 24 shared jobs surveyed were in the voluntary sector plus four in law centres. International Voluntary Service (IVS), the Royal National Institute for the Blind, the National Childminding Association and the National Council for Civil Liberties employed job sharers at this time. Over the years, voluntary organisations have continued to employ job sharers, largely on an ad hoc basis. Particularly where an organisation has very few, or in some cases, only one full-time post, job sharing is an excellent way of increasing the variety of skills and interests available as well as preventing the feeling of isolation experienced where there is only one full-time post within an organisation.

The list of organisations employing job sharers has continued to expand to include housing associations. Increasingly, voluntary organisations are formalising job-share policies and drawing up agreements. Oxfam and MIND have policies and a variety of organisations are now advertising jobs as open to sharers.

Save the Children Fund introduced a pilot scheme in 1985, and seven posts have currently been approved for sharing. Individual requests to job share after maternity leave were dealt with previously on an ad hoc basis.

Chapter 7

Employing Job Sharers

Why employers consider job sharing

The demographic changes and skills shortages are beginning to have a marked effect on the number and range of employers willing to consider job sharing.

The most frequently mentioned reason for employers to take on job sharers is that it can help them to retain skilled staff. This is why both Boots and British Telecom have introduced schemes.

In many cases, the specific cause for concern is the loss of women who do not return after maternity leave. One employer remarked:

> 'I became interested in the idea when I saw how many women, who had very good qualifications and who had been with us a while and whom we had trained, were leaving because they could not cope with both full-time work and a family. It seemed an awful waste and . . . an expensive loss for us if someone new had to be brought in and trained.'

It is also increasingly seen as a way of recruiting staff who for a variety of reasons are not able to work full time.

In the Institute of Manpower Studies (IMS) report on *Job Sharing in the National Health Service* (1989), 78 per cent of the authorities using job sharing gave the alleviation of recruitment and retention difficulties as a major reason for its introduction. The Industrial Relations Services (IRS) study of 37 job-share schemes in 1989 concluded that the most important reason for operating or starting a scheme is to retain staff.

Many of the formal job-share policies agreed by local authorities over the last eight years have been introduced as part of an equal opportunities package aimed both at helping women to remain in the career structure, as well as encouraging those with childcare responsibilities to return to work. A survey of 243 women returning to work after maternity leave, carried out by the Maternity Alliance in 1988, asked them to rate factors which might affect their resumption of work. Included in the top four was the right to return part time (79 per cent). However, the survey found that women returning part time are especially vulnerable to losing out on promotion prospects.

When Bristol City Council introduced its equal opportunity policy in 1984, it was conscious that its female workforce was concentrated mainly in the lower grades. Job sharing was developed as one means of removing some of the barriers to employing women. Since its introduction, the scheme has also become attractive in recruitment and retention terms. Although more employers are now introducing career-break schemes which allow people to take a break and return at a later date, for many the option to continue in their jobs after maternity leave, but on a less than full-time basis, suits their needs best. Job sharing can also help employers to retain and recruit people who have caring responsibilities for the elderly or other dependants; people with disabilities or health problems; and people studying or with other interests.

The benefits

1. A wide range of skills and experience

Two people sharing one job are likely to have different areas of specialised skill or knowledge which complement and reinforce one another, and which are unlikely to be available in one individual. In a survey of schools employing job sharers in Sheffield Education Authority, 'head teachers' views were that there were enormous benefits from having two teachers share . . . one post. Classes profited from having double the specialisation, skills, energy and expertise from two personalities.'

2. Increased energy, motivation and commitment

Late in 1982, a study of 20 alternate-week workers at Lloyds Bank was published in the *Employment Gazette*. Managers found the method of working very productive. Staff were 'cheerful, co-operative and responsive; extremely hard-working and conscientious, not prone to bad days'. One manager said that attitudes were better than among full-time staff:

'Alternate-week workers always try to get their work finished by Friday evenings. They take off less time than full-time workers and are generally more productive.'

Many employers have come to realise that job sharers are fresh, energetic and creative during the hours they are at work. This is confirmed by the views of job sharers themselves. In the 1980 EOC survey, the majority of respondents believed that employers do get more work out of two people doing a job. One explains:

'Both I and my job sharer do at least one and a half times the hours of work we're paid for. Half timers tend to work flat out without a tea break.'

These views are also borne out by Pritchard's 1988 study.

Jean Lammiman, who shared a job as Training Manager at the Stock Exchange, says of job sharers:

'We certainly compact more energy; we don't have so much wind-up and wind-down time as people working a full week.'

3. *Continuity*
One advantage of employing job sharers is that if one person is off sick or on holiday, at least part of the job can be covered; and if one person leaves, half the job is continued while a replacement is found.

4. *Flexibility*
It is possible for job sharers to work peak periods together or attend different meetings at the same time. A health authority considered one of the advantages to be: 'a little greater flexibility in spreading hours of work to cover peak times; for example, at out-patients clinics both doctors could attend.'

5. *Spin-off from outside interests*
The time spent in activities outside the job, some of them directly or indirectly related to the work, may bring new approaches and knowledge to the job.

The costs
Although there are extra costs involved in employing job sharers, as one local authority commented in its initial report on job sharing, 'The costs and benefits associated with job sharing are difficult to evaluate, these being mainly associated with the advantages and disadvantages outlined.'

The IRS survey (1989) found that most of the 37 organisations contacted felt the costs were marginal and outweighed by the benefits. The Incomes Data Services (IDS) study of six job-share schemes said that the comment made by BP International that 'although job sharing increases the number of staff, it does not increase costs' summed up the views of the organisations in their study. Boots the Chemist, for instance, believed that any increases in costs were minimal. Following her experience of employing job-sharing training officers in 1981, Rhiannon Chapman, Head of Personnel at the Stock Exchange, felt that 'there was no significant increase in cost involved in having two job sharers'.

1. National Insurance

Employers often assume that it will cost more in National Insurance (NI) contributions to employ two people rather than one. However, this is not the case: job sharers are treated individually for National Insurance purposes, and in most cases employers would save on NI contributions. Where employees are contracted out of the state pension scheme, the savings vary from £155 per annum where two people share a post which has a full-time salary of £6,000, to £590 per annum where the equivalent full-time salary is £20,000 (see Appendix 3 for details).

2. Administration

Although it will be necessary to administer two sets of wages and contracts, in practice, particularly where the payroll is computerised, the extra costs are likely to be minimal. Boots report that as they already have many part-time staff as well as people working on term-time contracts and variable hours contracts, administration is not a problem.

3. Training

Two lots of training are likely to involve both cost and time. Birmingham City Council suggest in their 'Guidelines to Management' that one way of lessening these is to invite both job sharers and their supervisors to an intensive induction process.

4. Accommodation

In many cases job sharers use the same desk, but an extra chair is often provided. Where individuals are in the office together for longer periods, an extra desk may also be provided – as is the case for Susan Williams and Sue Osborn, who share the job of Unit General Manager for Camberwell Health Authority. They both work Monday and Tuesday mornings, and overlap on Wednesday and Thursday lunchtimes.

5. Car allowances

Many employers now give each sharer the full lump sum car allowance if eligible, thus involving them in extra expense.

Potential problems

The most frequently mentioned problem areas relating to job sharing found in a New Ways to Work survey (1987) are overtime payments, blocking of promotion for full-timers and public holidays. In fact, many of these areas generally referred to as difficult are the result of lack of specific guidance on how to deal with the issues rather than being inherent problems.

Disadvantages which came to light in the Industrial Relations Services study of 37 schemes (1989) include other managers' hostility to a scheme, colleagues believing they would be over-burdened if they had to work with 'mere part-timers', other employees believing that the sharers were blocking a promotion path. One organisation reported a male backlash (defused by a trade union meeting); another found resentment towards sharers from older women who had not had such opportunities themselves. None reported substantial problems between sharers, although some thought this could be a problem.

Concern by employers that they may be left with half a job to fill seems not to be borne out in practice. Nevertheless, according to New Ways to Work, 'what to do if one partner leaves' is the most frequently mentioned anxiety of employers new to job sharing.

Factors some employers consider problems are seen as advantages by others. In a 1988 Industrial Society study of seven job sharers, which probed strongly on the 'perceived losses to the organisation', some employers thought that having two doing a complex job made it 'disjointed', for others it provided variety and flexibility. Although several factors were clearly important, in their view few were major (see Chapter 9 for further discussion of these issues).

Introducing job sharing

A policy or not?

In the early 80s very few organisations had formal policies on job sharing. The usual way for a job share to begin was for individuals to negotiate with their employers. There were also some cases of pairs applying jointly for posts (without being invited to do so) and being successful against competition from full-time applicants.

If a job share proved successful within an organisation then it was likely that others would follow. This was certainly the case with the House of Commons Library and International Voluntary Service – early users of job sharing, who later employed more sharers. However, even when an organisation ended up with a number of shared posts, this didn't necessarily mean that any formal policy developed. By 1987 the House of Commons Library employed 12 job sharers, but without a formal scheme.

Although in more recent years there has been a tendency for local authorities to draw up schemes, there are still authorities open to job sharing who are without schemes. The IRS survey concluded that more organisations are considering setting up schemes or investigating the possibility of doing so. Within the 37 organisations covered, many informal schemes may change to formal ones. In addition large employers not included in the survey already accept informal arrangements or are planning a formal framework.

In the case of the BBC, informal arrangements have existed since a production assistant's job in BBC Schools' Television was shared in 1979. A personnel circular set down guidelines for introducing and operating job sharing in 1986. However, this only has advisory status. The corporation is currently negotiating a formal agreement which will be incorporated into the staff handbook. Equal opportunities officers in the BBC's separate divisions promote job sharing and are keen to see it become more widely available.

It is important to bear in mind that introducing and negotiating a formal scheme with trade unions can be a lengthy and extremely time-consuming process. In one case, it took a local authority a number of years to reach agreement with the union concerned over the details of a scheme. In the meantime job sharing continued, but different departments developed their own ways of implementing it. If this situation does occur then it is helpful if individuals are allowed to job share for the duration: the people concerned are likely to leave otherwise.

Some employers have introduced pilot projects within one department or where job sharing applies to a certain category of job. Avon County Council carried out a pilot project within the Leisure Department, and when this proved to be a success a full scheme was extended across the whole county. However, a problem with pilot schemes is that it can be very difficult for people in other departments who wish to job share during the pilot period. This can seem very unfair, and if applied too rigidly may result in people leaving.

In the early days of job sharing, pilot projects sometimes applied to one post only, as when the Inner London Education Authority allowed Mike Trier and Joan Nicholson to share a teaching post in 1982 (see p. 18). After a successful year and a further pilot scheme involving 70 shared posts a full scheme was eventually introduced.

Now that job sharing has been proved to work, particularly in the public sector, employers are more likely to feel that they can take the risk of introducing full schemes. However, in the private sector, where experience of employer-wide schemes is more limited, pilot or trial schemes allow a more cautious approach until job sharing is more widely accepted.

Boots originally planned a pilot scheme in 1988 but senior managers were sufficiently enthusiastic about job sharing and worried about recruitment to launch the scheme nationally. The company developed its formal job-share scheme within its retail division (Boots the Chemist); it does not apply in other divisions, but could act as a model.

Since the Halifax Building Society's initial one-year pilot job share of a departmental manager's post, a formal scheme detailed in a staff circular has now been drawn up. This is part of a number of equal opportunities initiatives, which also include career-break and re-entry schemes.

British Telecom also ran a pilot scheme in Scotland before launching the option nationally in early 1989.

The practical details

1. Eligibility

Many organisations operating job-share schemes now consider all jobs in principle as open to sharing; others have restrictive schemes with jobs above a certain level not included. However, some schemes (for example, the one run by Gloucester County Council) which orginally restricted job sharing to lower grades, have now been revised to cover all grades.

Some policies clearly state which jobs are not included in the scheme: for instance, Hackney Council excludes trainee jobs, such as apprenticeships and residential jobs, where the council would have to bear the additional costs of providing accommodation for the second sharer. In its 'Guidance for Managers', Hackney lay down that:

'All other jobs, however, are open to job share, and you may not refuse a request to share on the basis of the type of job alone. That is not to say that you have to agree to any working arrangement that a prospective sharer may put to you. If someone suggests working arrangements that will fail in practice, do not agree to them. The policy simply recognises that almost any job can be shared if there is enough commitment on both sides to overcome practical problems through flexible working.'

Birmingham City Council state that:

'Exemption will only be granted where the operational requirements of the job mean that sharing is not practicable, eg if the job holder has to be residential on site it may not be appropriate for the accommodation to be shared – if however, there are two lots of accommodation available, then the job could be shared.'

Where all jobs are generally considered open for sharing and all the employer's job advertisements state that job sharers are welcome to apply, managers wishing to exempt a job from the scheme usually follow an agreed procedure. For example, Leicester City Council include a question in their general recruitment advertising form which asks: 'Please give your reasons why this job cannot be shared.' Camden Council, who have 148 shared posts and have had a full policy in operation since 1982, say that 'to date, no job has been identified by chief officers which has given cause to the Chair of the Women's Committee to recommend to the Staff and Management Services Committee that it is unsuitable for job sharing.'

Bristol City Council considered drawing up a list of exclusions at the beginning, but felt this to be too daunting a task. The policy now operates on the premise that job sharing is permitted except where the chief officer of the relevant department can prove to the satisfaction of union representatives that the post is such that the service provided by the council would suffer by the arrangement. If the exclusion of a post is contested by the union, the case will be heard by an appeals sub-committee composed of elected members.

A request to job share at a branch of the Halifax Building Society would be considered by the employee's manager in the light of the organisational requirements of the branch concerned. The manager's recommendations and the original application are then submitted to the regional office which is responsible for job shares. If the manager cannot recommend the job-share request, a full report is forwarded to the regional office. The staff member is then given full details of the reasons for the request being declined: the employee may still be able to place his or her name on the job-share register. The society's policy is to endeavour to comply with requests for job sharing but 'the overall implications must be beneficial both for the employee and the branch/department'.

In many organisations, any dispute over agreement of a post for job sharing is covered by the general grievance procedure. At Boots, the suitability of each particular job for sharing is considered individually, and so far there have been no unsuitable cases. If employees feel that they have been unfairly treated in terms of eligibility for job sharing, they may refer the dispute to the company's grievance procedure at area level. In some organisations a specific panel may be brought together to consider job-share grievances.

2. Leaving arrangements

This is generally considered one of the most difficult aspects of job sharing: what happens when one sharer leaves? The most common first step is for the remaining sharer to be offered the post on a full-time basis. If this is not acceptable then another partner is sought. The difficult question is what happens if, after a reasonable period (which varies up to six months), no partner can be found.

In most local authority agreements, if no partner can be found a full-time appointment may be made, and the remaining sharer is dealt with according to the council's redeployment procedure. Health authorities adopt a variety of replacement options: the most common of these is for the authority to attempt to find a replacement within a given period (redeployment or redundancy are retained as back-up options).

In the Institute of Manpower Studies' survey of health authorities, none of the case study respondents had experienced major difficulties in replacing sharers. Boots undertake to advertise the post for at least eight weeks. If, after the company has used its best endeavours to fill the post, no suitable applicant has been found, the existing partner will be offered the job on a full-time basis or another part-time post (even if this means a temporary downgrading). Boots feel this is necessary to maintain commercial viability. When they drew up their guidelines, this was a difficult issue to consider and the company was tempted to ignore the situation until it arose.

It can be difficult to find a partner if the job is specialised, and especially if it is a field in which few women are employed. However, it should not be assumed that it will be more difficult to recruit for a half post than a full-time post, even one at a senior level.

When Colchester Borough Council were advertising for someone to fill half the post of Assistant Chief Housing Officer, they were pleasantly surprised at the number and quality of responses to their advert. About three times as many applications were received as had been anticipated, and respondents were generally better qualified than those who had applied when the post was last advertised on a full-time basis.

Although there may be a problem in a sparsely populated area, in the small Welsh town of Aberystwyth, an advertisement for a job-sharing librarian in 1983 brought in 40 applicants.

Implementing a scheme

All organisations have their own procedures for introducing and developing new personnel policies; there is no one way. However, in its case study research into the ways in which local authority job-share policies were initiated, developed and implemented, New Ways to Work concluded that there were certain key factors which need to be considered by any employer introducing a job-share scheme. These include, first, the adoption of a formal policy statement. Unfortunately, some organisations feel that at this point they have done enough, but any such policy will then remain as a purely 'paper policy' unlikely to work in practice. Other steps which need to be considered include the following:

Trade union involvement
Full consultation between management and trade unions has been a key factor in the introduction of job-share schemes by local authorities. The National and Local Government Officers' Association (NALGO) was involved in negotiating the best possible terms and conditions for job sharers in many local authorities. Union involvement, although desirable, may not always be essential. Boots does not have a company-wide agreement with any union and so the scheme was not the subject of formal union consultation or agreement. However, there have been no objections from the Union of Shop, Distributive and Allied Workers (USDAW), which is recognised in some stores, or from the staff councils.

Central responsibility
When a policy and procedures for job sharing have been agreed, it is usually personnel officers and departmental managers who are

involved in the day-to-day implementation. In order to implement, monitor and review an organisation-wide policy effectively there must also be a central co-ordinator with responsibility for drawing up guidelines, organising any training and education sessions and to carry out overall monitoring.

Publicity

Organisations vary considerably in the extent to which they promote job sharing both internally and externally. Methods used include statements on job adverts, leaflets, articles in staff newspapers, information on internal job vacancy lists and application forms.

In some cases, publicity for a scheme is considered an integral part of its development. For example, Leicester City Council produce posters and leaflets which are widely distributed throughout the council offices; in addition, an extra sheet on job sharing is attached to the standard application form. Boots also produced a poster ready for the launch of their scheme (see p. 68), and the staff newsletter has carried articles about individual job shares.

Other methods used include staff memos and information sheets enclosed with pay slips. One council displayed the Hackney Job Share Exhibition in the civic centre for a week. Leeds Eastern Health Authority wrote to each member of staff informing them of the introduction of a job-share scheme.

The IMS study 'Job Sharing in the National Health Service' found authorities had a low key, ad hoc approach rather than a formal policy. Even some organisations who do have a formal policy do not actually publicise it in any way. Others only really make the option available to existing staff and do not include a 'job sharers welcome' phrase in external advertisements. Sometimes even members of staff may not know about the existence of a scheme; in one case, a woman found out about her council's policy by reading an article on job sharing in *Woman's Own*.

Guidelines

Guidelines or codes of practice which expand on the agreed conditions of service for job sharers can help to eliminate differences in the way a scheme is implemented. These are best drawn up at an early stage. Two councils who did not draw up detailed guidelines held meetings of job sharers after the schemes had been in operation for a number of years, and found various problem areas were highlighted. These were mainly caused by departments' interpreting conditions of service in different ways. Even within the same department, the scheme was operated differently between one building and the next. One particular problem area was the way in which bank holidays were worked out.

Training and education

Many of the councils where job sharing is an established part of personnel policy recognise the importance of general information and training sessions for individuals, managers and personnel officers. Without practical information on how job sharing works and how it can benefit them, managers may have negative attitudes to job sharing. As one local authority personnel officer puts it, 'When managers have done something one way for 99 years it is difficult to persuade them to change.' In order to implement a job-share scheme successfully, New Ways to Work's local authority survey found that it is vital to educate managers about the benefits and practicalities.

Some employers have run introductory sessions on job sharing for senior managers at an early stage in the development of a policy, in order to gain their support. At a later stage many now run sessions for line managers and personnel officers involved with implementing a scheme. Hackney Council regularly hold such sessions, which are run by Hackney Job Share. Boots held conferences for store and area managers at an early stage in their scheme. New Ways to Work also runs sessions for employers.

The Greater London Council (GLC) ran a series of training seminars about job sharing for staff sections and line managers. These half-day seminars comprised detailed lectures and training exercises on the Notes of Guidance, along with workshops dealing with recruitment, interviewing and selection of job-share applicants. They also included brief background information about the development of job sharing and examples of successful job-share arrangements at all levels in other workplaces.

These seminars were successful both in reassuring personnel officers about the viability of the scheme, by providing details of successful experiences in other authorities, and in clarifying various procedural questions relating to the day-to-day operation of the scheme. Specialists running the seminars were surprised to find a large number of misconceptions about the policy among officers, revealing the need for training in this field. Following these seminars, the volume of enquiries from staff sections to the Equal Opportunities Unit about job sharing considerably reduced.

(From *The Need for Job Sharing*, GLC Equal Opportunities Group, April 1986.)

Monitoring and review

Any new policies need to be monitored and reviewed to establish whether they are meeting their original aims. Where central personnel are monitoring other personnel policies, a number of questions on job sharing can be added to existing forms. The information which could be collected for a particular period includes:

- job sharers in post
- posts held by job sharers
- job-share applicants to advertised posts
- number of job-share applicants shortlisted
- enquiries about job sharing from full-time staff
- women choosing to job share on return from maternity leave
- jobs exempted from the scheme.

Other information could include the number of male/female job sharers and an indication of the grades of posts shared. Some organisations also monitor the numbers sharing broken down by ethnic group.

After a few years it may be helpful either to send a questionnaire to all job sharers or, as was the case with Leicester City Council, to organise a meeting so that job sharers can find out how the scheme is operating. This gives personnel staff an opportunity to review any aspects which are causing problems.

Birmingham City Council, who first introduced a scheme in 1983, carried out a full review after three years. There were very few shared posts (only 38 as at July 1986) and it was clear that some procedures needed improving, and that guidelines for managers should be introduced. The biggest change brought in after the review was that all jobs were declared open to job sharing, with an exemptions procedure to be followed if necessary. Guidelines were also produced, together with a poster and a leaflet for individuals. After this, the number of shared posts grew dramatically, amounting to 124 six months after the review was implemented, and over 200 by September 1989. The council are finding that more and more external applicants now tick the box on the application form asking if they want to job share, whereas to begin with most of the job shares agreed were internal requests.

Recruitment

The advertisement

Local authorities with job-share schemes now advertise them in a variety of ways. There is usually a phrase on job advertisements, such as 'job sharers considered', 'job sharing available' or 'job sharers welcome'. It helps potential applicants if adverts make it clear whether it is necessary to apply with a partner.

> Applications are particularly welcome from people with disabilities, from black and ethnic communities, women, lesbians and gay men. Job share applications are welcomed with or without a partner.

However, a large number of such phrases are in very small print at the bottom of the advert, and do not easily catch the eye. Southampton City Council place the phrase at the top of advertisements, where it is more easily seen:

> ### THIS JOB IS OPEN TO JOB SHARE
>
> ASSISTANT DIRECTOR OF HOUSING SERVICES (Finance and Administration)
>
> Salary within the range £21,003 to £24,813 (Pay Award Pending). (Actual commencing salary and maximum dependent on experience and responsibilities undertaken)

Where a general statement is made, such as: 'all posts open to job sharing unless otherwise indicated', then certain posts will have the phrase 'not suitable for job sharing' added. The London Borough of Kingston-upon-Thames has a special symbol which it places next to jobs which are available for job sharing:

> Job Share available where you see this symbol. Please tell us, when you apply, if you are interested in job-sharing.

If the post being advertised is a job-share vacancy, then similarly, it is important to make this clear:

WEST YORKSHIRE PROBATION SERVICE

PROBATION SERVICE ASSISTANT

(JOB SHARE) CITY COURTS, BRADFORD

These are some imaginative examples of adverts:

Barchester Health Authority
COMMUNITY UNIT

WOULD YOU LIKE TO JOB SHARE A SENIOR MANAGEMENT POST?

I am looking for a partner to share my post of Service Manager for people with a Mental Handicap, who is enthusiastic, self motivated, with a sense of humour and a clear vision of Community Mental Handicap Services.

Barchester has an intensive community development programme which will result in the closure of one hospital by 1991/92 and the substantial run down of another during the same period. I am determined to provide the best service possible for people with a mental handicap, within our resource constraints: consequently, you must have a high level of commitment to community services and be able to work systematically under pressure.

. . . .

If you have these abilities we can offer you not only a half-time job share, but also the benefits of a car leasing scheme, a generous relocation package (if appropriate) and a salary of c£16k pro rata which will rise with the new Senior Managers' pay arrangements.

```
┌─────────────────────────────────────┐
│          HOUSING SERVICES           │
│         'NEED A SHORTER             │
│            WORKING                  │
│            WEEK?'                   │
│                                     │
│     Then we have the following      │
│     vacancy for 18 hours a week.    │
│                                     │
│     Rents and Benefits Officer      │
│                                     │
│        Job Share arrangement        │
│   18hrs per week (Wednesday pm –    │
│     Thursday & Friday – can be      │
│            negotiable)              │
│                                     │
│   Salary: £6970.50 to £7362 p.a. inc. │
│            (pro rata)               │
│                                     │
│   We are looking for an enthusiastic │
│   and well organised Rents and      │
│   Benefits Officer to share responsi-│
│   bility for leading a Housing Benefit│
│   Team based in the Central Area of │
│   the Borough.                      │
└─────────────────────────────────────┘
```

The application form

Where job-share applicants are generally being encouraged, the standard application form should be adapted. This is often done by adding a box which has to be ticked. Leicester City Council enclose an additional sheet on job sharing, explaining the basis of their scheme; people interested in sharing fill in a tear-off slip.

Where and how to advertise

1. *Internally*

Where a job-share scheme exists, half posts can be advertised internally in the usual job vacancies' bulletin. To make it clear that job sharers are welcome in all posts, the employer may have to make some specific reference in the general information at the beginning of the bulletin.

For a large organisation, a register containing details of existing staff who would like to job share can be a good idea, but in some organisations a register is not considered an acceptable way of finding staff from the point of view of equal opportunities.

2. *Externally*

One of the problems in advertising job-share posts is that many people who would like to work in this way may have given up looking in the places where jobs are traditionally advertised. They do not expect to see adverts for part-time posts.

It may thus be necessary to try some more unconventional ways of advertising. If an employer is newly introducing a job-share scheme, then the local paper may be interested in a feature article, or the local radio in an interview (Boots and British Telecom have received much publicity in both the local and national press for their schemes). This helps generally to spread the word in the locality that a particular employer is open to flexibility and people are more likely to look at their subsequent job adverts.

(a) Newspapers and professional journals. It is now becoming more commonplace to see adverts for job-share posts, as well as for full-time posts stating that job sharers are welcome. People looking for job shares and more flexible working arrangements in the public and voluntary sectors in particular are likely to look in the *Guardian* appointments' pages. Adverts may also be placed in the local paper.

As professional jobs on a part-time basis have been very much the exception until recently, many people may not look in a professional journal. However, a number of professional associations are beginning to take specific steps to assist women members: these include the provision of career-break packs and reduced member-ship fees while on a career break (see Appendix 2).

As the use of job sharing spreads into more sectors and pro-fessions and generally becomes more acceptable, then people will feel it is worth looking in the professional journals. Journals which cover particular professions could well include a special column for job-share adverts. The Library Association tried this in the early 80s but at that stage it was not much used. In the future, this could be a very practical way for associations to help their members.

(b) Employment agencies. Some agencies have begun to specialise in the recruitment of job sharers or professional part-timers, for example Gemini Recruitment in Chelmsford (see Appendix 2 for addresses).

(c) Jobcentres. If Jobcentres are regularly used they may be willing to put up publicity material about the fact that all or some jobs are available for job sharing. Leicester City Council produced a card which was on display at Jobcentres.

(d) Networks. One way of reaching people who may not otherwise be looking at job adverts is to contact organisations such as:

> The Working Mothers Association
> Women Returners Network
> Women and Training

All these have regional/local groups (addresses are given in Appendix 2).

Adverts could also be displayed in local playgroups or schools.

Selection

In general, an organisation's usual procedures for shortlisting and interviewing will be followed.

Full-time posts

Some organisations will only consider people who apply with a partner. In this case they will be considered jointly alongside every full-time applicant. Some employers interview the sharers separately first, and then together. If the full-time applicants are allocated 30 minutes for an interview, then job sharers could be given 20 minutes each, followed by 20 minutes together, to consider the feasibility of a job share.

If a policy allows for sharers to apply either with or without a partner, a different procedure is needed. The following is that used by Camden Council.

> 'For all selection interviews each candidate is interviewed individually to assess personal ability to do the job. Applications who wish to be considered as job sharers:
>
> *(a)* Individual applications: they should be treated exactly as all others, then they should be assessed with each/every other person who has applied to job share (whether any of these applied jointly or not).
>
> *(b)* Joint job-share applications: they should also be treated exactly as all other candidates. They should then be assessed first with the job-share partner they have applied with, and second with each/every other person who has applied to job share.

Interviewers are perfectly entitled at the final stage to make any selection according to assessed ability, for example:

- to appoint an applicant for full time
- to appoint a joint job-share application
- to appoint one-half only of a joint job-share application either (*i*) with another individual job share applicant or (*ii*) with no other appointment, and then to advertise the other half
- to appoint a single applicant for job share and then as above.'

In Kingston-upon-Thames, guidelines state that 'job-share applicants should be interviewed individually in the first instance. Following individual interviews, job sharers should be given the opportunity to meet each other, together with the manager, prior to a decision being made to confirm the appointment.'

Job-share posts
The extent to which an existing job sharer is involved in the selection procedure for the vacant part of a post varies. One scheme sets out the following procedure in its guidelines:

'The remaining job sharer should be involved in any review of working arrangements and be consulted about the advertising stages, but not at the person specification or the selection or interviewing stage. The degree of consultation will obviously increase in ratio to the complexity and sensitivity of the duties and responsibilities of the post. The basic approach to person-alities should be that of professionals who are capable of working satisfactorily with any reasonable colleague.'

But what happens in practice? Although it is accepted practice that existing job sharers are not members of the selection and inter-viewing panels, they are usually given the opportunity to meet shortlisted candidates.

Gillian Lewis spent a whole day together with applicants as part of the selection procedure for the other half of her post as Assistant Chief Housing Officer in Colchester. She says: 'At least this gave us a chance to meet and talk to our potential job-share partners.'

Management issues

The role of line managers is particularly important in job sharing. Although all the managers interviewed in a recent study said that job sharing causes them extra work, practically all of them feel that the effort is worthwhile. The role and attitude of all types and levels of management are crucial: they strongly determine whether an individual job share succeeds or fails. Job sharers themselves acknowledge the importance of line managers, and generally feel supported by them. Job sharers are basically satisfied with the management of the job share by line managers, and see the line managers as crucial to the success of job sharing. Most line managers agree that supervising job sharers tends to be slightly more time consuming, but none thought the responsibility either too burdensome or too complex.

A study carried out by the Industrial Society of seven job shares (1988) found that job sharing required 'severe' appraisal of the way in which work is carried out and that it would probably lead to major adjustments affecting several other employees. Other studies by Incomes Data Services, Industrial Relations Services, the Industrial Society and New Ways to Work back up these findings.

The positive involvement of senior managers, particularly when a scheme is being drawn up, is important. One county council asked for comments on a discussion document produced by the personnel officer. However, the comments were not very positive and included: 'I applaud the view that job sharing in professional and managerial posts is an ideal; however, I do not see it as a practical option.'

In many cases, introductory information sessions can play an essential role in changing managers' attitudes. Many may have little information on job sharing, how it works and how they can benefit. As one personnel officer comments, 'The biggest problem is that people won't use their imagination about what a job share is.'

Oxfordshire County Council held a seminar on job sharing for senior managers at an early stage in the development of its scheme, and this can be a good way of allaying any fears which they might have.

Personnel issues

If an organisation decides to introduce a formal job-share scheme, personnel staff will be involved in extra work drawing up the details and organising procedures. In the early stages, this will require considerable input from the central personnel department. At a later stage when procedures are clearly set out, and as a scheme becomes established, departmental personnel staff and line managers will deal with its day-to-day running. The scheme at Boots is run at local levels, but the foundations were laid down in guidelines which were centrally produced. Once a scheme is established, involvement from central personnel is likely to be mainly in monitoring and review.

Some aspects of a job-share policy may conflict with aspects of an equal opportunities' policy (for example, recruitment and selection). It is important to look at any areas of potential conflict and decide how to deal with them at an early stage in drawing up a scheme.

Chapter 8

Employment Rights and Benefits

Employment rights

Job sharers are treated as individuals for the purpose of statutory employment rights. Thus under the Employment Protection (Consolidation) Act 1978 (EPA) all have basic rights to:

- equal pay for work of equal value
- protection from sex and race discrimination
- paid time off for ante-natal appointments
- protection from discrimination or dismissal for trade union activities.

For further rights, what counts is the numbers of hours worked and whether the necessary 'continuity of employment' can be established.

Employment rights for those working 16 hours or more a week.	
Rights	Qualifying period
Written statement of terms of employment	13 weeks
Maternity leave	2 years by 11th week before confinement
Maternity pay	2 years by 14th week before confinement
Unfair dismissal for pregnancy	1 year
Notice of dismissal	1 month
Written reasons for dismissal	2 years
Unfair dismissal	2 years
Redundancy pay	2 years
Time off to look for work after redundancy	2 years

Each person must normally work 16 hours or more each week, for a period of two years, or between 8 and 16 hours if they have worked for five years, in order to qualify for certain statutory rights. The rights which are affected by this are state maternity pay, redundancy pay and unfair dismissal.

Job sharers who divide their hours so that each person is working 16 hours or more every week will be covered. However, it is less clear whether continuity is established if you work uneven or alternate weeks.

Some employers allow employees certain rights under their terms of contract irrespective of the number of hours worked. Many organisations in the public sector award maternity rights which depend on a qualifying period, but not necessarily on any definition of continuous employment. Teachers employed by the Inner London Education Authority working less than 16 hours each week are fully protected for all statutory rights under the terms of their contract, except for protection against unfair dismissal, and this is made clear to them when they are appointed to job share.

Establishing continuity

Unfortunately, there is some ambiguity in the interpretation of the provisions in the EPA which govern continuity of employment. This is covered in Schedule 13 and broadly it is possible to say that weeks of employment will count if an employee:

- is actually employed for 16 or more hours (para 3); or
- works under a contract which normally involves 16 or more hours a week (para 4); or
- used to work under a contract which normally involved 16 or more hours a week, but now works under a contract normally involving between 8 and 16 hours, provided it is for no longer than 26 weeks (para 5); or
- works under a contract which normally involves 8 or more hours a week provided the employee has done so for five years continuously (para 6).

Temporary reduction of hours

A temporary or occasional shortfall in weekly hours will not generally break continuity because the word 'normally' means that tribunals look at the way a contract operates throughout its life. This is made clear in the case of the Secretary of State for Employment *v* Deary and Others (1984),[1] where dinner ladies who had been

97

employed for more than five years for at least 8 hours a week, had their hours cut to 7½ for two years. Here the tribunal found that during the life of the contract, the employment 'normally' exceeded 8 hours.

Three-day/two-day week working

If you have worked continuously for more than five years and the contract normally involved 8 or more hours a week, you will continue to be covered if in alternate weeks your hours are less than 16 hours. If you have been working for less than five years, continuity is likely to be broken. Because this way of working will usually mean that every other week you will not be working the requisite 16 or more hours continuity will be broken. In Opie *v* John Gubbins (Insurance Brokers) Ltd (1978),[2] the plaintiff worked three days (20¼ hours) one week and two days (13½ hours) the next, on an alternate week basis. The tribunal held that the plaintiff could not average out the hours because a 'normal' working week was not the same as an 'average' working week. 'Normally' meant regularly and there could only be the occasional shortfall.

One suggested way of securing employment protection rights for job sharers working uneven weeks is to ensure that the contract states that normal working hours are 16 plus each week – regardless of what actually happens in practice. In Rennie *v* Scottish Amicable Life Assurance (1982),[3] the tribunal said that if the contract 'lays down an obligation to work for a specified number of hours it is not necessary to inquire as to how many hours were in fact involved.' They said that only where there were no written terms was it necessary to look at the actual hours worked. However, the use of this 'device' has not been tested with job sharers.

Alternate week working

Week-on/week-off working seems to fall into a similar trap, because the 'week off' breaks continuity. In this situation, Schedule 13 paragraph 9(1) (c) preserves continuity where an employee is absent from work 'in circumstances such that, by arrangement or custom, he is regarded as continuing in the employment of his employer for all or any purpose'. A favourable decision was made in the case of Lloyds Bank Ltd *v* Secretary of State for Employment (1979),[4] where the tribunal held that a bank clerk working alternate weeks came into this category. They said that the weeks off amounted to an absence 'by arrangement' and so counted as periods of employment, coming within one of the provisos to the continuity rules, under Schedule 13.

However, this interpretation is open to serious doubt since the House of Lords' decision in Ford *v* Warwickshire County Council (1983).[5] Here they said that this proviso could only apply where the contract of employment had in fact ceased, and that would clearly not be the case in an alternate week arrangement.

Acquired rights

Paragraph 7 allows employees who have already qualified for a particular employment right to retain it even if their normal hours subsequently drop below 16. However this right is lost at a later stage if:

1. the contract normally involves less than 8 hours work a week, and
2. you actually work less than 16 hours in any week.

For many people, job sharing follows a number of years of working full time. In this circumstance one can say, broadly speaking, that you will continue to qualify for the statutory rights you have acquired as long as the job share involves at least eight hours a week. For example:

Sue works for 20 months at 37½ hours a week and then goes on maternity leave. Five months later she returns to her previous job, working 14 hours a week on a job-share basis. When dismissed a year later she can claim unfair dismissal.

Comment: Sue's maternity leave does not break her continuity of service and counts towards the two years' qualifying service needed. Thus under paragraph 7 her right to claim unfair dismissal is preserved, even though her weekly hours have dropped below 16.

In *New Work Patterns: Putting Policy Into Practice*, Patricia Leighton, a labour lawyer, states:

'For several years there have been doubts (though no directly relevant case law) as to whether job-share arrangements of a "week-on week-off" or "fortnight-on/off" nature ensure continuity of employment through the non-work period. Although it is not possible to be definitive, continuity is probably preserved either because the employee remains governed by the contract during non-work periods; or because the gap is clearly "temporary" in that the sharer will take over the work at the prescribed times. "Workless" days, or even a workless week, will not necessarily break continuity.'

Although the right to go to an industrial tribunal for unfair dismissal cannot be written into a contract, employees may still be able to sue their employers under the terms of their contracts for wrongful dismissal in the ordinary courts.

Some job-share agreements state clearly that job sharers must be made aware of possible loss of statutory employment protection rights if they are employed for less than 16 hours per week, and then the decision is up to them. However, others state that job sharers should not work less than 16 hours per week.

In Pritchard's study, 82 per cent of sharers were contracted to work 16 or more hours a week. Only 6 per cent had contractual hours of less than 16 per week and about 12 per cent were on temporary contracts – often of under one year (usually to cover maternity leave).

Building Businesses not Barriers

The government White Paper, 'Building Businesses not Barriers' (May 1986) proposed that the thresholds of 8 and 16 hours should be raised. The intention was to raise the 16-hour threshold to 20 hours, or for employees to work at least 12 hours a week for five years, in order to qualify for most employment rights. A very wide range of organisations lobbied the government on these proposals, which have not become law. In January 1989, the *Financial Times* quoted Mr Patrick Nicholls, Junior Employment Spokesman, as saying that the government had no immediate or longer-term intention of putting the proposals into employment law.

Terms and conditions of service

It is a basic principle of job sharing that sharers should receive pro-rata terms and conditions. Many aspects of the conditions of employment will be the same as for full-time workers, but it is important that matters specific to the job-share arrangement be agreed between employer and employee, either in the form of a collective agreement or included in the individual contract or both.

The contract

The law states that all employees working for 16 or more hours a week must be provided with a written statement within 13 weeks. Job sharers should each receive a separate contract of employment. Sheffield City Council's agreement states:

'Each partner to a job share will hold individual contracts of employment . . . The postholders' job title will be that given to the established post with the endorsement.' (*Job Share*)

Employers approach the issue of contracts of employment for job sharers in a wide variety of ways. Patricia Leighton and Catherine Rayner in their 1986 study found no examples of written job-share contracts in the 43 organisations they studied.

Employers have been unsure whether to adapt existing full-time or part-time contracts, or to devise a specific job-share contract. One job sharer when asked about her contract said: 'This is really a mess! We each have a contract stating we each work part time! Our organisation's contracts are pro-forma printed things which only give two options: full time/part time. One of these options has to be deleted – they don't seem to think to write in "Job sharing"! I've taken it up with the personnel department.'

The London Borough of Camden, who have had a full job-share policy and guidelines since 1982, have produced a rather lengthy document, in which relevant clauses are ticked and job sharers referred to the guidelines on specific points.

Another method is to issue job sharers with a letter setting out details, such as the minimum number of hours to be worked, minimum overlap time and what happens if one sharer leaves. The letter will then refer to the job-share policy and agreement, which is either attached or easily available for reference.

In some cases, employers have devised a specific job-share contract. An example of this is that produced by North Bedfordshire Health Authority.

Job Sharing: A TUC Guide includes a section on points which should be covered by a contract.

Conditions of employment
As a general principle, all conditions of service should be applied, where appropriate, on a proportional basis according to the number of hours worked (unless otherwise agreed).

The following aspects of conditions of service are likely to need specific consideration and some clear statement of how they will be dealt with.

Hours of work
Where a job is being divided equally, the statement that you will 'normally work X hours a week' would be the most straightforward

way of dealing with this (see page 98). In cases where jobs are not being divided equally it is important to consider whether, if one sharer leaves, the remaining hours would be a viable package to attract new applicants. If there is too great a difference between the hours worked by each partner, there is a danger that the person working the larger number of hours might become too dominant. The following is an example of a situation that could arise:

A and B were jointly successful in obtaining a job-share post, and wanted to divide the hours in such a way that A worked 16 and B worked 21. Both would be covered for employment protection purposes and 16 hours would be an attractive number of hours to advertise should A leave. The employer must be quite clear as to what would happen should B leave and A now want to increase the hours worked to 21. Would this be allowed, would A have to remain on 16 hours, or be asked to increase to 18½ hours so that the post is equally divided?

Rate of pay

The full-time wage is divided between the sharers pro rata to the hours each works. Where incremental salary scales apply, it is possible for job sharers to be on different incremental points according to qualifications and experience. Similarly, with performance-related pay scales sharers would usually be assessed as individuals, although some of the criteria may relate to their performance as job sharers. At Boots, sharers also have a pro-rata entitlement to the profit-sharing scheme.

Overtime pay

Overtime payment for part-time workers has always been a contentious issue. Should they receive overtime pay when they work more than their normal hours, or when they work more than the normal full-time hours? However, with job sharers the situation is slightly different. If the sharers together have already completed the full-time hours for that week and one partner is asked to work extra hours, at what rate should they be paid? In practice, this is not likely to be a major problem. Most job sharers will not want to work much overtime, and it may be a reflection of poor management if overtime is required; in addition, time off in lieu is often granted.

If either partner works over their standard hours for a particular week, then the job-share unit as a whole would exceed the normal 35- to 37-hour week, and thus it would not cost any more for the employer to pay for the extra worked at the overtime rate. One problem is that the payment of enhanced overtime rates for job sharers is difficult if part-timers are also being employed.

This issue has sometimes created problems. In Sheffield City Council, it significantly held up the signing of the agreement. Because the council would not agree to pay the overtime rate, the agreement now states that 'no job sharer will work overtime which involves the unit working over the contracted hours'.

Some employers pay the enhanced rate as soon as the work unit has exceeded 35 to 37 hours for the week, and do not see the issue as a problem. Others have agreed a compromise, where if sharers work more than their normal hours and if these hours are beyond the hours of the 'normal working day' or at 'unsocial hours', then overtime rates are paid.

Annual holidays

Holidays should be worked out on a pro-rata basis. Where the share is on a 50/50 basis this calculation is straightforward:

> A works five mornings and B five afternoons. The full-time holiday entitlement is four weeks. Both A and B get four weeks' holiday, but are paid at their usual rate of half pay for those weeks.

> C and D work a week-on/week-off arrangement. The full-time holiday entitlement is six weeks. C and D each get six weeks' holiday, but are only paid for three weeks.

Where the week is unevenly divided it is easier to convert the entitlement to hours. For example:

> A works 16 hours a week and B 21 hours. Full-time employees work 37 hours. Full-time employees are entitled to five weeks or 25 working days' holiday. Annual holiday entitlement will be:

Full-timer 5×37 hrs = 185 hours
A $\qquad\quad$ 5×16 hrs = $\ \ $80 hours
B $\qquad\quad$ 5×21 hrs = 105 hours

Bank holidays

According to New Ways to Work, what to do about a fair allocation of bank holidays between job sharers is one of the most often quoted 'problem areas'. As most bank holidays fall on a Monday, the difficulty occurs when one sharer always works on a Monday.

Again, the most straightforward way of looking at this is to work out the entitlement in hours. There are currently eight public holidays during the year, thus where the full-time working week is 35 hours, the full-time entitlement is 8 × 7 hours or 56 hours.

If job sharers are working on a 50/50 basis, each will be entitled to 4 × 7 hours or 28 hours. This amount can then be added to the annual holiday entitlement.

For sharers who work on Mondays, this means that because organisations are usually closed on bank holidays they will have to use up some of their annual holiday entitlement to cover for these days. One alternative if the organisation has a flexitime system is to make adjustments through flexitime debit or credit. In some organisations sharers have been left to work out an equitable system for themselves, but in others practice varies considerably. In some, a rather rigid approach has meant that sharers who usually work on a Monday have to work extra time within the bank holiday week to make up the half day less they have worked.

Long-service leave
Each individual should be entitled to long-service leave based on that individual's length of reckonable service.

Sick leave and pay
Entitlement to sick leave varies considerably and is usually related to length of service. Length of sick leave should thus be calculated individually according to length of service. If the full-time entitlement is six months on full pay and six months on half pay, this will be at a job sharer's normal rate of pay for the first six months and half the normal rate of pay (ie a quarter of the full-time rate) for six months. Where an employer does not contract to pay occupational sick pay, employees will be dependent upon Statutory Sick Pay (SSP) or state sickness benefit. All SSP payments made by an employer can be claimed back from the Department of Social Security (DSS) – you do not have to claim. The amount of SSP depends on weekly pay, not the hours worked.

It is important to reach agreement with an employer on what are known as 'qualifying' days, particularly where sharers work 2½ days a week or a week-on/week-off arrangement or uneven weeks. If normal working days only are agreed as qualifying days, some job sharers will lose out because they will have to wait longer before being entitled to SPP, as well as in most cases receiving less money.

It is best to get all five days of the week agreed as qualifying days or, where applicable to the job, all seven days. There will be no extra cost for the employer as SSP is claimed back from the DSS.

Maternity leave and pay
To be eligible for state maternity pay it is necessary to have been in 'continuous employment' for at least two years by the beginning of the 11th week before the expected week of confinement. Time off for maternity leave counts towards continuity. Many unions have negotiated more generous maternity leave provisions with employers, and job sharers should be eligible for maternity pay on a pro-rata basis. If you are returning to job share after maternity leave, then check what the agreement says on this: a period of notice is usually required.

Probationary period
If it is necessary for new employees to complete a satisfactory probationary period, each job sharer should be assessed individually. If one job sharer fails the period then the agreed procedure for recruiting another half would be used.

Interview and removal expenses
Job-share applicants should be entitled individually to these expenses in accordance with conditions for full-timers.

Car allowances
Practice varies on this point, but in general any casual car user's allowances will be paid on the usual basis, ie according to the number of miles travelled.

Lump sum car allowances
Some employers pay this on a pro-rata basis. However, many now pay any lump sum to sharers as individuals. Given that possession of a car is considered an essential part of the job, this recognises the fact that individuals will each have to buy and run a car.

Company cars
The Halifax Building Society allows for a 'pool' car to be shared by both partners; in another example, two women each have a Ford Fiesta instead of the large saloon which goes with the job. Another approach is to work out the value of the benefit and share that.

Training

The general approach to 'on-the-job' training is that it is allocated on an individual, rather than a pro-rata, basis. The attitude to off-the-job training varies, depending on whether the employee has been instructed to attend a course where time off will be given.

Flexible working hours

Most job-share schemes allow that where a post is covered by a flexible working hours (FWH) scheme, the terms of that scheme will normally apply. However, there are some examples where this is not the case and this is an issue which could be taken up by the trade union, as there would seem to be no good reason why job sharers should not be eligible for an FWH scheme.

Pensions

Traditionally, part-timers have not been eligible for many company pension schemes. This position is now changing (see Chapter 9 for further details and discussion of the pensions issue): the local government pension scheme now admits people who work 15 or more hours a week; the Boots scheme currently only allows people working 20 or more hours to join the scheme.

The conditions of service will usually detail arrangements for staying in, or joining, the relevant scheme if you are reducing your hours, or joining on reduced hours. Ask for full details of the scheme, and find out in particular if your working pattern will affect your eligibility. For example, in Scotland members of the local government pension scheme who work alternate weeks are not eligible, because it is necessary to work 35 weeks a year.

Conflict of interest

Many organisations issue contracts of employment which contain clauses restricting individuals' involvement in alternative employment that would lead to a conflict of financial interests or breach of contract. Job sharers who are considering setting up in business (and indeed any other employee) should look at such clauses carefully.

Promotion

It is usual to allow job-sharing 'units' to apply for promotion on equal terms with full-time employees. Some organisations only consider the sharers together, and either appoint or reject them both; others will consider them individually as well as together and appoint the 'best person for the job', so it may be possible for one sharer to receive promotion and not the other (see Chapter 9).

Considerations specific to job sharing

Agreement will need to be reached as to what will happen in the following situations (whether or not these points are covered in a specifically drawn-up job-share contract or in separate guidelines referred to in the contract, will depend on the employer):

Specific job responsibilities

Job sharers are jointly responsible for carrying out the duties and responsibilities of the job outlined in the job description. Some employers leave the division of responsibilities to the sharers and their manager, and this is not recorded as part of the contract. Others produce an addendum to the job description which sets out details of the way in which the job will be divided, as agreed at the interview.

Reasons for job sharing

It is generally accepted that the reasons a person has for job sharing are his or her own concern, unless there is a 'conflict of interest' (see above).

One partner leaves

It is important that there should be an agreement as to what will happen in this situation. The most common practice within local authority agreements is as follows:

- The hours of work previously undertaken by that job sharer are offered to the remaining person
- Another partner is sought, using the usual recruitment methods. During this period the vacant portion could be covered by the remaining job sharer, if willing, but at least half the post will be covered
- If no partner can be found within a reasonable period, the remaining sharer is dealt with in accordance with the employer's redeployment procedure (see Chapter 7).

The 'reasonable period' varies. One example is 'not less than six months from the last day of service of the previous job sharer and shall take account of the number of times the vacancy has been

advertised, being not normally more than two outside advertisements'.

One person is sick, on maternity/paternity leave or on holiday

Where one partner is absent from work for any reason, there should
be no contractual right to expect the other partner to cover.
However, the remaining person could be approached by the
manager and if willing may agree to work the extra hours and be
paid for them. It is important to remember that if one partner is off
then at least half the job continues, unlike the situation where a full-
timer is off.

Overlap time

Practice varies about whether anything is written into a contract or
an addendum to a job description about overlap time. In some cases
a specific reference is made, such as: 'Each sharer will work two
whole days and a half day, which will include an overlap of one to
three hours.' In others a general statement is made in the
agreement, such as 'where continuity is determined in the job
description addendum as an essential requirement of the job share,
such arrangement must be achieved within the normal established
total hours, where necessary reducing the work time span of
attendance'; or: 'The job description issued will be that prepared for
the established post with addendum to reflect agreements reached
at interview where overlap/continuity and/or split tasks are
required. The hours to be worked will be individually stated for each
partner to the job share. Total hours not to exceed established post.'

Accommodation

Where sharers divide the hours in such a way that they do not work
at the same time, or where overlap periods are for only a few hours,
it is usual to share a desk, with the provision of an extra chair.
However, where the sharers work together for a more substantial
period, an extra desk is usually provided.

Uniforms/Equipment

In the case of uniforms, for example for nurses, these can be
expected to last twice as long. Other equipment can usually be
shared.

State benefits

Unemployment benefit
If you become unemployed after a period of job sharing, you should be entitled to claim unemployment benefits provided:

- you have paid 25 Class 1 contributions in one of the last two tax years before the calendar year on which the claim is based
- 50 contributions have been paid or credited in each of the two tax years before the year on which the claim is based.

Maternity leave
In order to qualify, you must work for an employer who employs six or more people and have worked for at least 16 hours a week for the same employer for at least two years by the end of the 12th week before the baby is due (or if you work between 8 and 16 hours you must have worked for the same employer for at least five years). At least three weeks before you intend to leave, tell your employer in writing that you are taking maternity leave and that you intend to return. You may take up to 29 weeks after the baby's birth.

Statutory Maternity Pay
You must have worked at least 16 hours a week for at least six months for the same employer by the 15th week before the baby is due and you must earn at least the lower earnings limit (£43, 1989).

If you are not eligible for Statutory Maternity Pay or Statutory Sick Pay through your employer, you may be eligible for maternity allowance or sickness benefit. Further information is available in leaflets from the Department of Social Security, or contact your union.

Means-tested benefits
Income support. You may be eligible for income support, which has replaced supplementary benefit, if you and your partner (if you are a couple) work less than 24 hours a week.

Family credit. You may be eligible if at least one partner, or a single parent, works more than 24 hours a week, and has at least one dependent child.

Housing benefit. Even if you don't receive the above two benefits, you may still be eligible for housing benefit.

Even if you are not entitled to the above benefits, you may be eligible to low income entitlement to free prescriptions, dental treatment and sight test (see leaflet AB11 from the Department of Health).

Contact a Citizens' Advice Bureau or Advice Centre for further information.

References

1. Secretary of State for Employment *v* Deary and Others (1984) IRLR 180.

2. Opie *v* John Gubbins (Insurance Brokers) Ltd (1978) IRLR 540.

3. Rennie *v* Scottish Amicable Life Assurance (1982) EAT 243/82.

4. Lloyds Bank Ltd *v* Secretary of State for Employment (1979) IRLR 41.

5. Ford *v* Warwickshire County Council (1983) IRLR 126.

Chapter 9

Other Considerations

Pensions

A little over half the total workforce belong to an employer's pension scheme. However, the number of part-time employees in pension schemes only represents 13 per cent of the part-time workforce. Full- and part-time woman employees stand to gain important new rights under their company pension schemes when the 1989 Social Security Bill becomes law. The Bill contains provisions which under European Community law must implement equal treatment principles for men and women in occupational schemes no later than 1 January 1993. The Bill outlaws indirect discrimination, which means that companies will no longer be able to deny part-timers access to their pensions schemes if most of the part-time workers are women.

A European Court ruling in the case of Bilka-Kaufhaus found that the exclusion of a part-time woman employee from her firm's pension scheme breached Article 119 of the Treaty of Rome. Employers can only justify different treatment if they can show economic reasons for the distinction. A number of companies are already changing their pension schemes to include part-timers, for example the Midland Bank, the Royal Bank of Scotland and Sainsbury's.

Many occupational pension schemes create problems, particularly for people who want to job share as a way of easing the way to retirement. Schemes operate in a variety of ways: in some, the level of pension is based either on the employee's final salary, or the best annual average in a number of consecutive years over the last, say, three years. You will need to find out how your employer's pension scheme operates.

Since 1985, the local government superannuation scheme has allowed people working 15 or more hours a week to join or remain in the scheme. Reducing your hours will reduce your benefits, but you do get what you pay for. For example, if you had worked full time for 24 years and half time for six years and your full-time equivalent salary at retirement was £10,000, you would receive a lump sum of £10,125 (compared with £11,250 if you had remained full time). Your annual pension would be £3,375 (compared with £3,750).

Promotion

About 21 per cent of the job sharers questioned by Pritchard (see page 8) had tried to get promotion as a job sharer, and of these almost exactly half were successful. All promotion attempts (except for two) were in organisations where there was an equal opportunities policy. Successful promotions were usually as a team, with a known partner within the organisation. One was promoted by appointment into the vacant half of a job share, and one was promoted on her own as a job sharer.

In the Industrial Society study, many sharers recognised that gaining promotion as a job sharer was likely to be extremely difficult, though job sharers can be promoted into full-time posts. Promoting job sharers, either singly or jointly, is a complex area. A highly competent job sharer ought to be able to gain promotion, and pressure will grow as job sharing itself becomes more common. This aspect will clearly have to be addressed by employers if job sharing is to become more popular.

Most of the sharers in the study felt that job sharing jeopardised their progress, despite theoretical opportunities and apparent equality of treatment. Where there were formal reporting or appraisal procedures, they were applied to the job sharers on an individual basis. There were no formal assessments of the job share itself in the study, and there was no evidence that managers thought it necessary.

Increasingly, however, employers are appraising the job-share element. Boots state in their guidelines for managers that:

'Each job sharer must be appraised as an individual. However, it will have to be made clear to the job sharer at commencement of employment that she/he will also be appraised on the level to which the job-share arrangement is effective. Merit will be awarded looking at an individual's performance on both these counts.'

New Ways to Work report that there are now more examples of job sharers being successful in gaining promotion together.

After Frances Wheat and Maggie Jones had been sharing a

planning job for Westminster City Council for two years, they decided that they needed new challenges. Over a period of a few months they applied for three posts, attended three interviews and obtained one job offer. Since September 1987 they have worked as a Principal Planning Officer (PO4) for the London Borough of Hillingdon. This is the joint covering letter which they sent when they applied to Hillingdon:

Dear Sir,

Principal Planning Officer – Projects

We are enclosing our application forms for joint consideration for the above post. We have been job sharing together for two years and have successfully demonstrated that the arrangement can work in a managerial position, and now feel ready and able to move on to a more responsible and challenging role. We have not felt it necessary to make the case for job sharing or to point out its many advantages, especially to the employer, but we would be happy to clarify any practical details if required.

Individually we are both qualified to undertake the duties of the post, but together we would bring a greater breadth of work experience and skills than any one individual could bring to the position. Our wide-ranging experience has given us an insight into the complete mechanics of the development process and the possible roles of public, private and voluntary sectors.

Yours faithfully,

Margaret Jones and Frances Wheat

Number of people sharing one post

Some employers keep an open mind over the number of people who can share one post. There are examples of one post being shared between three people. For example, three museum security staff each working 12 hours a week share one job in the Arts Department at Bristol City Council. In such cases it is important that people are aware of how their pension and employment rights are affected.

Another option is for three people to share two jobs, or five people four jobs. Some of these arrangements are allowed for within an overall job-share policy, for example, three community workers share two jobs in Sheffield.

Is there a saturation point?

It is unlikely that large numbers of people within an organisation will want to job share at the same time – it is a choice which the majority will not want, or be able, to make. In the London Borough of Camden, where there has been a job-share policy for seven years, 3 per cent of the workforce are job sharers. In Bristol City Council the figure is 2.4 per cent, and in Sheffield City Council 1.3 per cent.

However, within certain departments or teams there may come a point where a high percentage of the team is working on a job-share basis and any more shared posts could become a problem. The difficult question is, who decides if saturation point has been reached and using what criteria? In the New Ways to Work survey of local authorities (1987) one personnel officer suggested that rather than waiting for this point to be reached, a fair approach could be as follows: if a team/section feels that saturation point is likely to be reached in the near future, a case could be made, stating that if any more applications to job share were received from existing employees these could not be accommodated within the team; other possibilities, such as transfer to another team, should be considered.

A policy may not be enough

Even if an employer has a job-share policy and agrees to an existing member of staff job sharing there may still be problems. One sharer explains:

'Almost anyone can opt for job sharing in my local authority – it is now very difficult for a request to be turned down. There are some who support it, but my immediate seniors only pay lip service to it, and don't appear to see its benefits; they regard my request as being awkward. It's over a year now since I gave my three months' notice/request and was accepted to share my full-time post; but I still have no partner. The day before I was due to start job sharing my seniors hadn't lifted a finger about either finding a partner or making a management decision on how the work was to be spread. I was asked, "Could you delay job sharing for a bit?" I answered, "No, I've already made personal arrangements."

'My workload with no partner is the same as for parallel officers, except that two projects were taken off me. During the year I have managed quite well to do far more than 50 per cent of the post's work. Last week when I explained I hadn't had time to read a report for comment, I was told, "Take it home, it makes nice easy reading in all your spare time."'

The benefits of persistence

Susan Barnard has been sharing a planning officer's post with St Albans District Council for the last four years, and during this time she has shared with three people. In 1985 she put her name on the Royal Town Planning Institute (RTPI) register of unemployed planners as willing to job share and was approached by Phillida who was also on the register. Both were members of the professional institute, and they decided to look for a full-time planning assistant's post together. They applied for a job with Camden, who had a job-share policy, but were unsuccessful. Although St Albans did not (and still does not) have a job-share policy, they were appointed together as the best candidates for the job, even though the attitude to job sharers was not positive. Susan had been out of planning for about four and a half years, although she had recently taken a temporary full-time job for a month; Phillida had been working more recently. They were appointed at the top of salary Scale 5. Although Susan was accepting a job at a lower grade and salary than her qualifications and experience merited, she was delighted to have got the job.

After a while the two put in for regrading, as they felt that with their years of experience they should be on a higher grade. In fact, this coincided with an internal vacancy; they applied for and got a job on the Senior Officer grade, but were put on the lowest spinal point. Shortly afterwards, the department introduced career grades in order to attract staff. Junior and less experienced staff were being appointed at higher points on the scale, so eventually they were put up one spinal point.

When a job as Deputy Team Leader was advertised, Susan and her partner put in for this, but were told they would not be interviewed. After a while the job was advertised again, and they applied once more. When they found that they were not being interviewed they asked why: they were told it was not thought that job sharers could do the job and they would need to convince the chief officer otherwise.

Not wanting to give up, Susan phoned the RTPI for examples of other planning job shares at higher levels. The two were put in touch with planners in Bristol, who had taken up a grievance over this issue on the basis that it was indirect sex discrimination, and they obtained a copy of the statement which had been used in this case.

Susan and her partner looked at their own council's equal opportunities policy and wrote to the director of personnel. With no further discussion, they then heard that they would be interviewed. The other two candidates did not turn up for the interview and they were given the job. Again, they felt that it was very much the case that they were appointed because there was no one else and they were better than nobody! In spite of four years' dedication and loyalty and no major problems, Susan feels that the job share is still not seen in a positive light.

Susan and her partner are now on grade SO2 and are Deputy Team Leader in a team of eight people. If the team leader is away, they deputise and are responsible for five members of the team; they have not experienced any problems with this. With the current regrading in the department, they expect to be regraded to Principal Officer level along with other team leaders next year.

The job is in development control, dealing with planning applications. Because it provides a service to the public, it is important that the week is completely covered. In order to have a day in the officer together, each sharer works three short days. One works Monday, Wednesday and Thursday; the other Tuesday, Wednesday and Friday. They divide the cases between them and don't hand over work from one to the other. The main shared responsibility is the supervisory role.

Is there a right to job share?

Although there is no legal right to job share, a refusal to allow part-time working can lead to claims of indirect discrimination under the Sex Discrimination Act (1975) on the basis that proportionally fewer women can comply with the requirement to work full time. To succeed in a complaint of indirect discrimination, a woman has to show three things:

- that the employer has applied a requirement or condition to her which would equally apply to a man, but
- the proportion of women who can comply with it is considerably smaller than the proportion of men who can comply with it, and
- it is to the women's detriment because she cannot comply with it.

The complaint will then succeed, unless the employer can show that the requirement is justifiable irrespective of sex.

There have been a number of cases over the last few years where women claimed indirect discrimination over their employers' refusal to allow them to work part time or job share after maternity leave. The first case was Holmes *v* The Home Office (1984).[1] Ms Holmes, a single parent employed as an Executive Officer by the Home Office, had had her request to work part time after the birth of her second child refused. Both the Industrial and Employment Appeal Tribunals held that she had been indirectly discriminated against on the following grounds:

- Knowledge and experience suggest that large numbers of women between the ages of 24 and 40 are engaged in bearing children and looking after them and consequently cannot work full time
- The employers were not justified because recommendations of the Kemp-Jones Report and the Joint Review Committee of the Whitley Council supported the case for part-time work. The evidence of these reports was extremely valuable for Ms Holmes
- They accepted that Ms Holmes could not comply with the requirement because of her parental responsibilities and the excessive demands which would be placed on her time and energy.

It was made clear at the Employment Appeal Tribunal that the case was decided solely on the particular facts before it. Although not intended to set a precedent, this case has led to a number of cases being brought by women wanting to job share/work part time. In each case, the following questions must be considered:

1. Is full-time working a requirement of the employer or the job?

It is more often than not conceded that a requirement or condition, ie insistence on full-time work, has been applied. However, in the case of Clymo *v* Wandsworth Borough Council (1987),[2] the tribunal looked at whether working full time was a requirement or condition imposed by the employer as part of the very nature of the job itself. Here they felt that it was for 'the employer, acting reasonably, to decide – a managerial decision – what is required for the purposes of running his business or his establishment'. New Ways to Work feels that this part of the decision is particularly worrying because it suggests that where a post is at a more senior level working full time is part and parcel of the job itself, not a condition of the job, and a case would fail without the employer's even having to establish justifiability.

2. Is the proportion of women who can comply with the requirement to work full time 'considerably smaller' than the proportion of men?

In the Holmes case the Tribunal did not call on statistics but accepted that 'it is still a fact that the raising of children tends to place a greater burden upon them than it does on men'. There are no firm rules about the appropriate 'pool' for comparison, the only statutory guidance being that the comparison must be made between people who are not in materially different circumstances.

The definition of the 'pool' can bring different results. In Fulton *v* Strathclyde Regional Council (1983),[3] 100 per cent of the male social workers worked full time and 90 per cent of the women could have met the requirement to work full time. The tribunal held that 90 per cent was not a 'considerably smaller' proportion. However, in Robertson *v* Strathclyde Regional Council (1985)[4] the pool used consisted of all qualified careers officers in Scotland. The tribunal accepted that the almost equal number of men and women employed in the careers service represented only 55 per cent of qualified women, but 96 per cent of qualified men, and that this difference meant that a considerably smaller proportion of women could comply with the full-time requirement than men.

3. Can the employer justify the requirement to work full time?

The onus of proof is on the employer. The employer must show 'objectively justified grounds', as laid down by the House of Lords in an equal pay case Rainey *v* Greater Glasgow Health Board (1987).[5] The employer must show that there was a 'real need' for the requirement, that it is 'appropriate with a view to achieving the objective in question and necessary to that end'.

In Greater Glasgow Health Authority *v* Carey (1986),[6] the tribunal accepted that a requirement for health visitors to work every day, though on a part-time basis, was discriminatory, but held that it was justified. They accepted that there was substantial evidence that health visitors needed to be available five days a week in order for an efficient service to be provided. 'Administrative efficiency' was specifically mentioned in the Rainey case. The health visitors in the Carey case had wanted to work two whole days and one half day.

In Prince *v* University of Manchester (1986),[7] the tribunal rejected the university's argument about problems of sharing where the nature of the work was private and confidential (it involved a job in the salaries and wages section) but accepted that the responsibility of supervising staff could not be shared.

In the Clymo case, the tribunal again accepted that the employer was justified in refusing the application because it was a supervisory post. They accepted that the job of branch librarian required absolute consistency of approach and involved the supervision of junior staff. The council's case was that they encouraged job sharing provided the conditions were right. The tribunal considered that the council 'reached a managerial decision in a reasonable and responsible manner'.

Opposition in principle to job sharing is very unlikely to provide an adequate justification. In the case of Hicks *v* North Yorkshire County Council (1985),[8] the council had expressed reservations about dividing a teacher's post into two 'as there may be difficulties in obtaining a suitably qualified teacher in this area on a part-time basis'. The tribunal found that the council's objection was simply 'a matter of principle, nothing less and nothing more'. In Guthrie *v* Royal Bank of Scotland plc (1986),[9] the bank had refused to let a woman return part time after maternity leave on the basis that it was not their practice, and work methods could not accommodate such staff. The tribunal took the view that 'a relatively minor adjustment' was all that was required, and the bank had failed to justify the 'full-time only' policy.

4. Is the full-time ruling to the employee's detriment?

In the case of Holmes the Tribunal accepted that it was, without requiring specific evidence, and this line had been followed even in otherwise unsuccessful cases without argument. It must be shown that the requirement or condition operates to a woman's detriment 'because she cannot comply with it'. The test is whether she can in practice comply, not whether there is a theoretical possibility of compliance: convenience is not enough if it is practicably possible for her to comply with the full-time requirement.

In the Clymo case, the Tribunal did not accept that Ms Clymo 'could not comply with the requirement' but considered it was a 'personal preference not to'. In coming to this decision they had taken into account the joint salaries of herself and her husband, the availability of childminding facilities locally and the fact that the council had offered childcare.

In 'The legal context to job sharing', New Ways to Work takes the view that the line taken in these cases is not very satisfactory for many employees who wish to insist on job sharing or working part time.

> 'There is no scope for men to bring a claim, nor for women who want to job share for some other reason apart from the care of children. Even for women who can fulfil some of the criteria there are especial difficulties if the job involves supervising others and/ or is at a senior level, as the employer will most probably be able to claim justifiability. On the whole the picture of a successful claim is where the job is at a lower level, there are a lot of women already working part time and the tribunal takes a somewhat paternalistic attitude to the onerous duties facing working mothers.'

Although very few claims have reached industrial tribunals, there is some evidence both from the Equal Opportunities Commission and New Ways to Work that the very possibility that an employer may be taken to an industrial tribunal has resulted in employers' agreeing to requests to job share before they reach this stage.

References

1. Holmes *v* The Home Office (1984) IRLR 299.

2. Clymo *v* Wandsworth Borough Council (1987) EAT/487/87.

3. Fulton *v* Strathclyde Regional Council (1983) EAT/949/83.

4. Robertson *v* Strathclyde Regional Council (1985) COIT S/3332.

5. Rainey *v* Greater Glasgow Health Board (1987) ICR 129.

6. Greater Glasgow Health Authority *v* Carey (1986) EAT/745/86.

7. Prince *v* University of Manchester (1986) COIT 1840/211.

8. Hicks *v* North Yorkshire County Council (1985) COIT 1643/117.

9. Guthrie *v* Royal Bank of Scotland (1986) COIT 31796/86.

Chapter 10

Trade Union Involvement

Early involvement

Trade union responses to the issue of job sharing have been variable. Initially, very little attention was paid to the idea. Traditionally, unions had not had much to do with part-time workers, owing to the difficulties of organising them and fears that part-timers might be used to undercut full-timers' rates of pay. The reasons why many unions did become more involved is indicated by the following comment from a trade union official:

> 'The union wasn't too interested in job sharing at first. But what happened is we have all these individual members around the country negotiating their own individual agreements without union help. So we've had to start looking at it.'

Because of the development of job sharing in a number of local authorities in the early eighties, the National and Local Government Officers' Association (NALGO) was the union most active in its promotion as an equal opportunities measure. Nationally, NALGO recognised job sharing as 'an exciting development in part-time work' in its booklet 'Rights of Working Parents: a negotiating kit' published in 1981.

Another union with an early involvement in job sharing was the National Association of Probation Officers (NAPO), who passed a resolution at their national conference in 1981 calling for job sharing to be pursued locally by branches. A number of branches, for example in Inner London and Greater Manchester, were involved in local negotiations.

By 1981–82, interest was being shown in job sharing as a possible solution to the unemployment situation. In June 1981, GEC Telecommunications introduced job sharing for young people at its Coventry Works: this was in response to the fact that 73 per cent of young people in the Coventry area were unemployed. In January 1983 the government started its own 'Job Splitting Scheme', with a £338,500 advertising campaign.

Under the scheme, employers received a £750 grant for every job split. When the scheme was announced it was condemned by the TUC, the Equal Opportunities Commission and New Ways to Work. The main argument against it was that whereas job sharing aims to open up reasonable jobs for those who want to work part time, job splitting was aimed at people wanting and able to work full time but who cannot find a job. It was restricted to the unemployed and those receiving benefit or under a redundancy notice, and was clearly aimed at reducing the unemployment figures. As it turned out, the scheme was not a success, and even after some small modifications in the summer of 1983, take-up continued to be slow: between January 1983 and March 1987 only 1,563 applications were approved. In April 1987 the scheme was relaunched as Jobshare, but it has still failed to reach its targets and a year later only 522 applications had been approved.

The announcement of the Job Splitting Scheme came at a bad time from the point of view of union involvement in job sharing. Many unions were beginning to be more positive, but the scheme caused confusion. The TUC, NALGO and many other unions came out very strongly against the scheme. The TUC condemned the Job Splitting Scheme as discriminatory against women and a crude attempt to camouflage unemployment and remove employment rights. In March 1983, NALGO circulated all branches nationwide with information stating the difference between job sharing and job splitting.

Antagonism towards job sharing continued to be felt in the trade union movement, but as Lil Stevens, President of the National Union of Public Employees (NUPE), said in an article in 1984:

'There is no contradiction in trade unions' taking up the issue of job sharing and ensuring that employees' rights are safeguarded, while recognising that it is not the answer to the problems of the vast majority of women seeking employment or better conditions. It is one more element in opening up the range of opportunities, particularly for women, which the trade unions should not turn their backs on.'

In 1985 the Executive Council of NUPE agreed that job-sharing initiatives were to be welcomed as opening up higher paid jobs to people who wished to work part time, provided that satisfactory agreements could be reached to safeguard the interests of job sharers and other staff. NUPE's policy statement puts job sharing in the wider context: 'Job sharing is not seen as a substitute for campaigning and negotiation to reduce working hours for all staff;

to improve pay, conditions and status for part-time staff; and to improve the provision of childcare facilities.'

The National and Local Government Officers' Association (NALGO)

A large number of NALGO branches have been involved in negotiating agreements with local authorities. In *Job sharing: negotiating guidelines*, published nationally in 1986, they aim to answer key questions and map out strategies for negotiating a workable and imaginative job-sharing agreement. The booklet states that the advantages and safeguards negotiated for sharers can often be used as a lever to hitch up the rights of other part-timers. In a survey of 38 local authorities with formal job-share policies carried out by New Ways to Work in 1987, union support had been received in all but three of the councils. NALGO had initiated the policies in a quarter of these, in most cases jointly.

The Sheffield City Council branch took part in the very detailed negotiations leading up to the signing of an agreement with the council in 1983. In Sheffield, all applications to job share need NALGO approval; this was included in the agreement as a way of ensuring that terms and conditions agreed by different departments were kept to branch standards. A checklist is filled in by local shop stewards, and approval is given by the service conditions officer.

In December 1986 the branch called a lunchtime meeting of job sharers, which was attended by over 100 people. Following this meeting a job-share working group met regularly and drew up job-sharing guidelines for shop stewards. An education day school for shop stewards where the guidelines were talked through was also held at the end of 1987. The seven-page document points out the potential advantages and drawbacks for employer and employee: it also sets out the procedure for setting up a job share.

Teaching unions

Teaching unions have been involved with job sharing since the early 80s, although not always by supporting it. The Inner London Teachers' Association (ILTA) were involved in negotiations with the Inner London Education Authority in 1982–83. They were basically in favour of the introduction of job sharing, but opposed the initial scheme on two grounds: first, that it did not apply to all posts, as headships and deputy headships were excluded; second, the scheme made no provision for the payment of overlap time. The ILTA sought payment of half a day each week for sharers at scale one, which would have meant a total extra cost of £30,000. Overlap time was initially rejected as unnecessary, but later on this was accepted in principle.

When Sheffield Education Authority announced its job-share policy in 1982, the Sheffield Association of the National Association of Schoolmasters/Union of Women Teachers (NAS/UWT) wrote to the *Times Educational Supplement* saying, 'We will counsel our members strongly against participating in the scheme.' Seven years later the NAS/UWT has produced a national policy statement for LEAs on good practice in implementing job sharing for teachers, to ensure that its members' interests are protected when such schemes are set up. The document makes it clear that the union does not oppose job-sharing schemes, as they are of particular value for women with domestic responsibilities, who find it difficult to pursue a career as well as raise a family. A word of warning, however, was given by the union's general secretary, Mr Fred Smithies: 'Unfortunately, job-sharing schemes could become a convenient vehicle for unscrupulous employers to cut jobs and increase workloads in order to save money.'

The National Union of Teachers (NUT) produced notes of guidance on job sharing in 1984 and is now in the process of producing a leaflet. In spite of the many success stories of job sharing in teaching, the annual conference of the National Association of Head Teachers in Wales in 1989 defeated a proposal that local authorities and governing bodies should, where practicable, encourage job sharing in schools.

Six teaching associations in Surrey were reported as being against a job-sharing scheme announced in Surrey earlier in 1989. They think it will lead to an inconsistency in approach by job sharers in the classroom, as well as poor communication in record-keeping.

The National Association of Teachers in Further and Higher Education (NATFHE) have negotiated agreements on job sharing in a number of branches, and nationally the union has included an information sheet on job sharing in its Part Timers Campaign pack. In November 1984 the Association of University Teachers (AUT) agreed a policy statement on job sharing.

The Trades Union Congress (TUC)

The 1983 Women's TUC reaffirmed its support for job sharing for those who choose to work part time, and asked the Women's Advisory Committee to draw up guidelines to help unions negotiate job-share arrangements. However, it took a number of years before agreement could be reached on these and they were finally published as *Job Sharing: a TUC Guide* in 1988. The guidelines aim to help trade union negotiators and individual trade union members to take advantage of the possibilities of job sharing, while avoiding the pitfalls. They stress that they are not intended to divert attention from the need for unions to negotiate better rights for all part-time workers: 'While job sharing is an attractive concept, in practice it can have many disadvantages and can put employment rights at risk. It is essential therefore for trade unions to be fully involved from the outset in all job-sharing arrangements in the workplace.' The guidelines advise that no agreement should be signed before the following matters are resolved:

- Job sharing should only be introduced following adequate trade union consultation, according to properly negotiated agreements
- Trade unions should have control over the scheme at all times
- Job sharing must not involve replacing full-time workers by part-timers
- Job sharing must be voluntary
- Job sharing arrangements must be offered to current employees before external applications are invited (but care must be taken to avoid discriminatory advertising)
- Job sharing should not be used as a trial period for employment
- Potential job sharers should be advised to contact their union representative before entering into job-sharing agreements, so that they are aware of the full implications of job sharing before they make final decisions. Attention should be drawn to implications for pensions and for unemployment benefit.
- Each job sharer should work over 16 hours per week in order to qualify for employment rights
- Each job sharer should have an individual contract of employment.

At the TUC Women's Conference in March 1989 a composite motion on 'Flexible Working and Career Breaks' was passed. This called upon the TUC to encourage individual unions to prioritise flexible work arrangements in their negotiations with employers, including job sharing, career breaks, maternity and paternity leave and paid leave for care of dependants. In addition, the conference also asked the TUC to organise a survey of unions on all these matters with the results to be reported back in 1991.

How unions can help

At national level, unions can play an important role in producing general information and guidelines on job sharing. In 1989 the health service union COHSE (Confederation of Health Service Employees) produced a briefing and guidelines on job sharing. These state that 'COHSE supports the introduction of job sharing as an equal opportunities measure.' They also state that 'It is vital that COHSE officials are involved in every stage of the setting up of job-share schemes. We must ensure full consultation and achieve the implementation of schemes which are beneficial to our members.'

The National Union of Journalists' (NUJ) Equality Council have produced a leaflet on job sharing, which contains a model claim for an agreement. At the *Financial Times*, the NUJ chapel was involved in drawing up the agreement and one of the book publishing branches is actively involved in negotiations.

In a booklet 'Part-time Working – a TGWU Shop Steward's Handbook' the Transport and General Workers' Union includes a section on job sharing. It states that 'As far as the TGWU is concerned job sharing is valuable in giving the opportunity to work part time to people who cannot or choose not to work full time.' It lists a number of important points to bear in mind and refers to the TUC guidelines for further information. In 1987 the TGWU launched a campaign to recruit part-time and temporary staff. In February 1989 Bill Morris, Deputy General Secretary, said that flexibility had been considered a management tool, but unions had to accept that many women wanted to work part time to cope with family responsibilities; bargaining agendas had to be adjusted accordingly.

Although the Banking, Insurance and Finance Union (BIFU) don't have any national policy, a number of branches are currently involved in negotiations with some of the major banks. The Association of Professional, Executive, Clerical and Computer staff (APEX) issued a pamphlet 'Less than full-time working' in 1987, aimed at informing part-time workers on their legal position. A section on job sharing points out that the union must be satisfied that the quality of employment is protected and that no posts, or part posts, are lost by using job sharing.

The National Communications Union (NCU) were involved in 1988 in negotiating a framework agreement on job sharing with British Telecom. It is up to branches to negotiate detailed agreements locally.

As a result of declining union membership generally, many unions have been making specific efforts to recruit women members. At its annual conference in June 1989 the General, Municipal, Boilermakers' and Allied Trades Union (GMB) agreed that it would no longer negotiate pay and conditions on the assumption that the average employee is single, mobile, without responsibilities and will have an uninterrupted working life. The union, which has been trying to negotiate agreements including childcare and flexible working hours, agreed to review its internal structures to further increase the participation of women members.

An example of how a local union can play an important part in negotiating an agreement is the case of the NUT and Kent County Council. Initially, the Equal Opportunities Panel of the Kent NUT organised a one-day conference in an attempt to persuade Kent to become an equal opportunities employer. Following this, a working party on career development for women was set up and a policy document produced; this included provision of a job-sharing scheme available to teachers up to and including deputy head level. It was identifiably different from part-time teaching in that each job share is filled as a 1.1 full-time post, with the extra 0.05 for each sharer to be used as liaison time and not for class contact time.

Union involvement at early stages in negotiations with employers can ensure that job sharing is available for jobs at all levels. For example, Strathclyde Regional Council had originally wanted to restrict job sharing to basic grade posts, but NALGO successfully held out for the policy to cover all posts. In Bristol City, the council proposed that the lump sum car allowances should be paid pro rata, but the union successfully won the right for sharers to the full allowance each.

Even where a union has a positive policy on job sharing for its own members, it does not necessarily mean that people who work for that union are able to job share themselves. In some cases, union staff members have found it impossible to negotiate job shares. However, NALGO staff have been able to job share under an agreement signed in January 1986.

Unions can negotiate improved access to pension schemes for part-timers. After many years of campaigning, NALGO won the right for part-timers working 15 or more hours a week to be members of the pension scheme. BIFU has taken two banks to Industrial Tribunals over their refusal to include part-time staff in their pension schemes.

Unions can also help by negotiating improvements in a job-share policy and providing information for members. In Sheffield, the education authority defined its policy in 1982, and in June 1983 the Sheffield NUT Equal Opportunities Group held a meeting on job sharing attended by over 50 people; it was recognised that the NUT should be more involved in negotiations, and that more information should be available to members.

Union post sharing

The National Union of Journalists has agreed job sharing for elected posts within the union. On its 1984 National Executive Committee it had four people sharing two newly created seats. In 1989, two women shared the presidency of the union. The leaflet gives details:

'NUJ members can stand jointly for a union post and share the workload between them. For example, two people can share the position of branch treasurer or chapel clerk. Post sharers:

- have the right to attend and speak at all relevant union meetings
- share one vote between them (if they disagree, they must abstain)
- count as one when a quorum is needed
- must resign if one vacates the post for any reason.

Two people may share the role of delegate to the Annual Delegate Meeting (ADM) but only one can be present at any time. Extra costs must be met by the delegating body. Post sharing does not apply outside the union, for instance at the TUC or the International Federation of Journalists conference.'

How to involve your union

Ideas for involving your union in the issue of job sharing are as follows:

1. Find out if your local branch has had any discussions on the issue

in the past, and if the union nationally has any policy on the subject (if necessary by contacting the union headquarters yourself).

2. Some unions have equal opportunities sub-committees or women's groups who can produce an initial report to be considered locally by the union.

3. Get involved in setting up a working party to look at job sharing and other flexible working arrangements – this could also consider negotiating an improvement of clauses in the collective agreement which discriminate against part-time workers.

4. Suggest that any weekend schools on equal opportunities generally include a session on job sharing or flexible working. A number of NALGO regions have done this. The NUJ held a workshop on job sharing and flexible working at its Women's Conference in 1989.

5. You could get your union to sponsor and organise a seminar on job sharing.

6. Even if your workplace already has a job-share agreement, there will probably still be scope for improvement. Many employers review a policy after a few years, and it will be important for the union to be involved in the review process. The union can also take up any grievances from people whose request to job share is refused and generally make sure that conditions of service for job sharers are fair.

Unions, like employers, are changing their attitudes on job sharing. They are beginning to recognise that job sharing can be a positive option for some of their members, and that they can play an important role in negotiating good conditions. Many of the manual, craft and other unions operating in traditional male areas have felt that job sharing is not an issue relevant to their members. However, in some cases this is changing, particularly where job sharing as a way of easing into retirement can be appreciated. Hackney Council, at the request of the craft unions, have changed their pension arrangements to link their job-share scheme with early retirement.

Chapter 11

The Future

Many people, who use job sharing as a way of reducing the number of hours in which they do paid work, have found that it has improved their quality of life. One GP said:

'I'm quite sure that I want to go on job sharing as long as I can, because I've made the discovery that I actually enjoy clinical practice much more when I'm not doing it full time. Life is short and I have too many things to do, so at present I don't want to go back to being a full-time GP.'

Some people have also discovered that the quality of their working lives improves, because sharing a job with another person can result in a new way of working, involving co-operation and collaboration, and less competition.

If job sharing is to work, the agreement and acceptance of senior and line managers, trade unions and other members of the workforce are needed. Although it is becoming more accepted, there is still a long way to go. As one manager involved in introducing job sharing commented: 'It's all about attitudes: if everyone wants to make it work, it will. The general attitude is to leave things as they are.'

However, largely due to demographic changes and skills shortages, attitudes are beginning to change. Job sharing is being introduced as one of a range of more flexible work options. On its own it is a limited option, and only a possibility for a small percentage of the working population. Other reduced time options are needed to fit people's desires more accurately in terms of the number of hours they would like to work in a job.

One person who previously shared a job managed to negotiate a working week which suits her:

'I've now negotiated a 28-hour week which gives more money, but still makes childcare possible. However, I work for a very sympathetic organisation, and this arrangement does cause problems as we now have a one-day-a-week job left, which is not very satisfactory for another person. Really, two people to one job is not ideal; three jobs shared by two people would be better, but in the end I think the emphasis should be flexible/shorter/different work hours rather than a tradition of a 35- to 40-hour a week "job" being shared.'

Unfortunately, in this country people have very little choice over the number of hours they work. From an individual's point of view, ideally each person could be given the opportunity to work the number of hours they choose over, say, a period of a year, with the option to change at the end of that period.

In the USA, some organisations are giving their employees this kind of choice. The original model for voluntary reduced work time options (V-time) was developed in California by a public sevice union. It was negotiated as a means of providing interested employees with less than full-time work schedules. A survey of union members found more interest in shorter hours than in higher pay; in the words of a union official, 'We wanted the programme as a benefit for our members. Our people wanted more personal time.' A typical V-time programme offers:

- a variety of reductions of work time (and pay) ranging from 2.5 per cent to 5, 10, 20 and 50 per cent
- maintenance of all employee benefits, pro-rated where necessary
- time off, either on a regular basis, in the form of the reduced day or week, or in a block of time as extra vacation or days off work.

Participation in the programme must be authorised by a supervisor and the schedule remain in force for a defined period, usually six or twelve months. This provides both employees and employers with an option to try out the new arrangement, in the assurance that the commitment has a time limit and can either be renegotiated or terminated at the end of that period. The essence of V-time is that it offers full-time employees a wide range of time–income trade-offs, enabling them to reduce work hours without jeopardising their full-time status. It can give employees almost limitless flexibility to balance work with their other needs, such as family, school, adapting to an injury or health problem, phasing into retirement. It also allows people to take time off to upgrade skills or when making the transition from one job or career to another.

In New York State 1,225 people are currently taking advantage of a scheme which allows them to reduce their hours by between 5 and 30 per cent of full-time working. The current participation rate is

1.9 per cent compared to a 1.6 per cent rate in 1985. The scheme was first offered in 1984 and has been extended several times.

In Sweden, parents can choose to shorten their working day to six hours during the first seven years of their child's life. If it is possible to organise this sort of choice for parents, why can it not be widened to include others?

There are no schemes in this country which allow people to reduce their hours of work in this way. However, some individuals are working reduced work-time arrangements, by individual negotiation with their employers. Paul Rathkey, a trade union researcher noted in an article in 1984:

> 'There is full-time work and part-time work and little in between . . . it seems rather ironic that in Britain there is widespread acceptance that options producing extra income through extra-time working (overtime) should be available (unlike most of its European counterparts where legislative limits, often strict – are set), but that options on reduced working time and voluntary reduced income should not be available, and should somehow be socially unacceptable.'

He concludes that:

> 'There is a growing recognition that individual workers want more choice in regard to working time and that they wish to work hours that suit them regardless of whether their union recommends it. Sooner or later the trade union movement is going to have to face up to these developments seriously. If the British trade union movement is to be seen by its members, and not just itself, as socially progressive, policy will need rethinking and changing.'

A more common consensus to move in the direction of changing work patterns is beginning to be felt in our society. Change will require the backing of government, employers' organisations and trade unions. Although much of the current interest is due to skills shortages and demographic changes, these are presenting us with an important opportunity to rethink the full-time work ethic.

Appendices

Appendix 1

Bibliography

Alston, Anna and Miller, Ruth *Hours to Suit* (Rosters, 1989)

Angier, Margaret *Job Sharing in Schools: an account of a policy in practice* (Sheffield Paper in Education Management No 40, Sheffield Polytechnic, 1984)

Curson, Chris ed *Flexible Patterns of Work* (Institute of Personnel Management, 1986)

Department of Employment *Women and employment: a lifetime perspective* (HMSO, 1984)

Equal Opportunities Commission *Job sharing: improving the quality and availability of part-time work* (1981)

Equal Opportunities Commission *Local authority equal opportunity policies* (1988)

Greater London Council, Equal Opportunities Group *The Need for Job Sharing* (1986)

Hurstfield, Jennifer *Part-Timers Under Pressure* (Low Pay Unit, 1987)

Incomes Data Services *Job Sharing* (Study 440, August 1989)

Industrial Relations Services *Job Sharing Survey* (Employment Trends 441, June 1989)

Lathlean, Judith *Job Sharing a Ward Sister's Post* (Ashdale Press, 1987)

Leighton, Patricia and Rayner, Catherine *Job Sharing in South-East Essex* (Essex Employment Relations Research Centre, 1986)

Leighton, Patricia and Winfield, Marlene *Does Job Sharing Work? Case studies and practical guide* (The Industrial Society and Essex Institute of Higher Education, 1988)

Leighton, Patricia and Syrett, Michel *New Work Patterns: Putting Policy Into Practice* (Pitman, 1989)

Meager, Nigel, Buchan, James and Rees, Charlotte *Job-Sharing in the National Health Service* (Report No 174, Institute of Manpower Studies, 1989)

NEDO/Training Agency *Young People and the Labour Market* (1988)

NEDO/Training Agency *Defusing the demographic timebomb* (1989)

NALGO *Job Sharing: Negotiating Guidelines* (1986)

New Ways to Work *Job Sharing: employment rights and conditions* (1988)

New Ways to Work *Job Sharing: putting policy into practice* (1987)

Pritchard, Mary *A Survey of Job Sharing* Unpublished, submitted as part of MA degree at Birkbeck College, London University, 1988)

Sorby Barbara and Pascoe, Maureen *Job Sharing: the great divide* (Leeds Polytechnic, 1982)

Syrett, Michel *Goodbye 9–5* (Newpoint, 1985)

TUC *Job Sharing: A TUC Guide* (1988)

Further Reading from Kogan Page

Humphries, Judith, *Part-Time Work*, 2nd edition (1986)

Reed, Alec, *Returning to Work: A Practical Guide for Women* (1989)

Steiner, Judith, *How to Survive as a Working Mother* (1989)

Wallis, Margaret, *Getting There: Jobhunting for Women* (1987)

Yate, Martin John, *Great Answers to Tough Interview Questions*, 2nd edition (1988)

Useful Organisations

Job sharing

Equal Opportunities Commission
Overseas House
Quay Street
Manchester M3 3HN
061-833 9244

Hackney Job Share
380 Old Street
London EC1V 9LT
071-739 0741
Aims to promote job sharing within the borough of Hackney. Have
an exhibition for hire and two videos on job sharing for hire or sale

New Ways to Work
309 Upper Street
London N1 2TY
071-226 4026
An independent organisation promoting flexible working patterns,
including job sharing. Has a range of publications for individuals
and employers

Regional job-share contacts

Manchester Area Jobsharers
31 Chandos Road South
Chorlton
Manchester M21 1TH
A voluntary group, working to promote job sharing throughout the
Greater Manchester area

Ann Wood
Sheffield Careers Service
AEU Building
Furnival Gate
Sheffield S1 3HE
0742 735461
Keep a job-share register on open access in the Careers Service Library

General

Working Mothers Association
77 Holloway Road
London N7 8JZ
071-700 5771
A self-help organisation for working parents and their children, which provides informal support through a network of local groups

Women and Training Group
c/o Ann Cook
Hewmer House
120 London Road
Gloucester GL1 3TL
0452 309330
Is committed to promoting the training and development of women, and has regional groups. It encourages companies and other employers to improve training opportunities

Women Returners Network
Margaret Johnson (Secretary)
Garden Cottage
Youngsbury
Ware
Hertfordshire SG12 0TZ
0920 464337
Aims to promote education, training and employment opportunities for women returning to work

Professional Associations

British Dietetic Association
c/o Karen Sorenson
Lewisham and North Southwark Health Authority
Guy's Hospital
St Thomas's Street
London SE1 9RT
071-955 5000
Preparing an information pack for returners, to include information
on job sharing

Arthur Moore
British Medical Association
BMA House
Tavistock Square
London WC1H 9JP
071-387 4499
Run a job-share register

British Paediatric Association
5 St Andrews Place
London NW1 4LB
071-486 6151
Run a job-share register

Chartered Society of Physiotherapy
14 Bedford Row
London WC1R 4ED
071-242 1941
Have a job-sharing pack

Chartered Institute of Public Finance and Accountancy (CIPFA)
3 Robert Street
London WC2N 6BH
071-930 3456
Have produced a career-break information pack advising on taking
a long break; returning after maternity leave; part-time working, job
sharing etc

Housing Employment Register and Advice
8th Floor
Artillery Row
London SW1P 1RX
071-889 3122
Produce a vacancies bulletin, which includes job-share and part-time posts. Run seminars on job sharing

Institute of Physics
47 Belgrave Square
London SW1X 8QX
071-235 0016
Publish a career-break kit, which includes information on job sharing

Institute of Housing
9 White Lion Street
London N1 9XJ
071-837 4280
Organise return-to-work scheme

The Library Association
7 Ridgmount Street
London WC1E 7AE
071-636 7543
Publish a booklet, 'Job-sharing'

Royal Town Planning Institute (RTPI)
26 Portland Place
London W1N 4BE
071-636 9107
Run a job-share register and keep information on job sharing for planners

Women in Medicine
7c Cassland Road
London E9
Publish a booklet, 'Job Sharing in General Practice'

Recruitment Agencies specialising in promoting job sharing and part-time work

Chelmsford area
Gemini Recruitment
run by June Saltmarsh
Robjohns House
Navigation Road
Chelmsford, Essex CM2 6ND
0245 492879

High Wycombe area
Share Recruitment
15 Warren Drive
High Wycombe
Bucks HP11 1EA
0494 439750

Thames Valley area
In Tandem Recruitment
56 Chapel Street
Marlow
Bucks SL7 1DE
0628 890819

Central London
Part Time Careers
run by Julia McIndoe
10 Golden Square
London W1R 3AF
071-437 3103

West London area
Clockwork Recruitment
run by Carol Jackson
112 Brunswick Road
Ealing
London W5 1AW

North West London Area
Unique Returners
766 Finchley Road
London NW11 7TH

Appendix 3

National Insurance (1989)

All figures are in pounds and pence. It is assumed that both job sharers do half the work and therefore receive half the pay.

Not contracted-out employers (no company pension scheme)

Salary per week		Employers' NI contribution				
Full time	Job sharer	Full time	1 Job sharer	2 Job sharers	Extra cost	Saving
81.98	40.99	5.74	Nil	Nil		5.74
82.00	41.00	5.74	2.05	4.10		1.64
104.99	52.49	7.35	2.62	5.24		2.01
105.00	52.50	9.45	2.62	5.24		4.21
139.98	69.99	12.60	3.49	6.98		5.62
140.00	70.00	12.60	4.90	9.90		2.70
154.99	77.49	13.95	5.42	10.84		3.11
155.00	77.50	16.20	5.42	10.84		5.36
209.98	104.99	21.94	7.35	14.70		7.24
210.00	105.00	21.94	9.45	18.90		3.04
305.00	152.50	31.87	13.72	27.44		4.43
309.98	154.99	32.39	13.95	27.90		4.49
310.00	155.00	32.39	16.20	32.40	0.01	
610.00	305.00	63.74	31.87	63.74		0.00

Contracted-out employers (who have a company pension scheme)

Salary per week		Employers' NI contribution				
Full time	Job sharer	Full time	1 Job sharer	2 Job sharers	Extra cost	Saving
81.98	40.99	4.18	Nil	Nil		4.18
82.00	41.00	4.18	2.05	4.10		0.08
104.99	52.49	4.92	2.19	4.38		0.54
105.00	52.50	7.02	2.19	4.38		2.64
139.98	69.99	8.84	2.40	4.80		4.04
140.00	70.00	8.84	3.80	7.60		1.24
154.99	77.49	9.62	4.04	8.08		1.54
155.00	77.50	11.87	4.04	8.08		3.79
209.98	104.99	15.52	4.92	9.84		5.68
210.00	105.00	15.52	7.02	14.04		1.48
305.00	152.50	21.84	9.49	18.98		2.86
309.98	154.99	22.36	9.62	19.24		3.12
310.00	155.00	22.36	11.87	23.74	1.38	
610.00	305.00	53.71	21.84	43.68		10.03

Figures courtesy of New Ways to Work

Index